John Hill Martin

Martin's Bench and Bar of Philadelphia

Together With Other Lists of Persons Appointed to Administer the... Vol. II

John Hill Martin

Martin's Bench and Bar of Philadelphia
Together With Other Lists of Persons Appointed to Administer the... Vol. II

ISBN/EAN: 9783337003388

Printed in Europe, USA, Canada, Australia, Japan

Cover: Foto ©ninafisch / pixelio.de

More available books at **www.hansebooks.com**

THE CAMERONIANS.

A Novel.

BY

JAMES GRANT,

AUTHOR OF
'THE ROMANCE OF WAR,' 'OLD AND NEW EDINBURGH,' ETC.

IN THREE VOLUMES.
VOL. II.

LONDON:
RICHARD BENTLEY AND SON,
Publishers in Ordinary to Her Majesty the Queen.
1881.

CONTENTS OF VOL. II.

CHAPTER		PAGE
I.	'A WEAK INVENTION OF THE ENEMY'	1
II.	CECIL RECEIVES HIS CONGÉ	11
III.	IN THE PRINCE'S STREET GARDENS	24
IV.	A FRUITLESS TASK	42
V.	THE REGIMENTAL BALL	53
VI.	HEW'S TRIUMPH	61
VII.	'I HAVE COME FOR YOUR SWORD	80
VIII.	THE COURT-MARTIAL	104
IX.	A PAGE OF LIFE TURNED OVER	116
X.	GONE!	128
XI.	'THE INITIALS'	141
XII.	TURNING THE TABLES	167
XIII.	BY THE MORAVA	190
XIV.	A MYSTERY	210

Contents.

CHAPTER	PAGE
XV. ON DUTY	220
XVI. THE CASTLE OF PALENKA	235
XVII. MARGARITA	247
XVIII. CAPTAIN GUEBHARD	262
XIX. THE BLACK MOUNTAINEERS	285
XX. CECIL COMES TO GRIEF	297

THE CAMERONIANS.

CHAPTER I.

'A WEAK INVENTION OF THE ENEMY.'

HEW resolved, as before, to lose no time in putting Sir Piers on his guard; he would give him an 'eye-opener,' he thought; and, in his ignorance of military discipline and etiquette, almost conceived that the baronet, as full colonel of the regiment, might have power to issue, perhaps, some very stringent and crushing order concerning the culprit.

Hew, among other 'caddish' tastes and propensities, was fond of 'sherry-glass flirtations ' at bars and buffets, where sham smiles are bartered for button-hole flowers, amid bantered compliments and honeyed small-talk, not always remarkable for its purity; and while engaged in one of these little affairs, he made the casual acquaintance of Herr Von Humstrumm, the regimental bandmaster, a somewhat obese-looking German, with an enormous moustache and his scrubby dark hair shorn remarkably short; and from the latter he drew—or alleged to Sir Piers that he drew—some account of the family and antecedents of Cecil Falconer; and with these he came home highly elated; and whatever the conversation really was, the communications did not suffer diminution in his relation of them; and he broke the matter to Sir Piers in a cold, hard, and exultant way, that could scarcely fail to strike the latter as being, at least, ungenerous.

' I have discovered who and what our hero is !' said he.

' Our hero—who ?'

'Our late visitor and guest, Mr. Falconer.'

'Captain Falconer. Well ?'

'I met the bandmaster the other day, at a luncheon-bar, and he told me all about him,' continued Hew, laughing immoderately.

'I know that in Scottish regiments, especially, every man's family is usually known, his antecedents, and so forth.'

'And *who* do you think this Falconer proves to be ?' asked Hew, with malignancy flashing brightly in his parti-coloured eyes. 'A pauper with a long pedigree, you will say. No, by Jove! he has not even *that !*'

'What *do* you mean, Hew ?' asked Sir Piers, looking up from his chair, with knitted brow.

'I mean,' replied Hew, 'he may, like the street balladers, sing

'"I never had a father,
        I never had a mother,
    I never had a sister,
        I never had a brother,
    For indeed I'm nobody's child !"'

And adopting the tone and manners of a street-singer, Hew gave this verse with extreme zest and almost fierce exultation, acting the part with such broad vulgarity that his hearer winced; but well did Hew know that he was bringing the strongest argument to bear upon the weakest point in the character of Sir Piers—an inordinate pride of birth and family.

'Good God! you don't say so, Hew?' exclaimed Sir Piers, more sorrow than anger predominating in his mind for a time—but a time only.

'Fact, though,' replied Hew, carefully selecting a cigar from his silver case, 'if a certain chain of deductions may be trusted, and I know that the thought of his obscure birth is gall and wormwood to him—have seen him blush for it more than once, at Eaglescraig.'

'His father——' began Sir Piers.

'Nobody knows who that illustrious individual was. I suppose he doesn't know himself, though he must have had one.'

' And his mother ?'

' Was a singer, or actress, or something of that kind. Folks in the musical world, like folks on the turf, all know something of each other, and so this fellow, Von Humstrumm, assured me that—that it is all as I say; and thus his excellence as a singer and pianist is accounted for at once. The Herr told me that he had performed at her private concerts given in the house of a noble lady in Belgravia, when the inner drawing-room was turned into quite a beautiful *bijou salon de concert*, and even royalty was present. Pretty circumstantial that !'

' Extraordinary !'

'Not at all ; there is nothing extraordinary in this world. Thus I should not wonder if the fellow once figured before the footlights ! Gad, if the Cameronians only knew of this, they'd put him in Coventry—force him to quit !'

' Then how the devil does this band-master come to know, if *they* don't ?' said Sir Piers, pacing the room in great annoyance of spirit. 'I don't understand all this! Was he not a Sandhurst cadet?'

'I don't know, and don't care,' responded Hew, with an access of sullenness.

'He certainly seems a finished gentleman!'

'I have heard you admire his hands as being white and shapely,' said Hew, with a sneer.

'Yes; but what of that?'

'Did you ever observe his mode of gesticulating with them?'

'No.'

'Well, *I* have, and to me it seemed to indicate foreign blood and player-like proclivities.'

Hew's hands were neither white nor shapely, and certainly bore no indication of that refinement of race on which his listener set such store.

'We have not heard the last of this fellow,' he resumed, after a pause.

'The last! What do you mean?'

'His interference in our family affairs. A card-playing fortune-hunter, as I denounced him to be before ; he was here no longer ago than yesterday afternoon, pursuing his designs upon our soft-hearted, and I must say, remarkably soft-headed, Mary ! I felt inclined to chuck him through the window. Must not this matter be stopped, sir, and with the strong hand ?'

'Stopped ; I should think so. Should he attempt to cross me, he'd better touch the fuse of a live shell !' replied the old man sharply, while memory went back to the bitter times when his young Piers, so loved, petted, and prized, forgot the high traditions of his family, and daringly linked his fate with a humble girl, whom the proud baronet declined to receive or recognise, most unwisely, as he thought at times now.

'We are an old family, Hew,' he resumed, after a pause ; ' and you will be the inheritor of my title in an untarnished condition ; but you must not rest upon it alone, and, with Mary's money added to what I have to leave you—Eaglescraig, wood and wold, tower and manor-place—

great things may be achieved. You will cherish Mary when I am gone, even as I have cherished her; for I have nothing else now,' he added, as he thought of his dead son and the never-to-be-forgotten night of the dread and shadowy vision.

'I cannot persuade her to enter even into a preliminary and formal engagement with me,' said Hew, after another pause.

'But,' urged the general, polishing his bald head with fidgety irritation, 'surely, by this time, something is understood?'

'That—that she will one day be my wife?'

'Yes, of course.'

'But when?'

'When I issue *the order!*' said Sir Piers, as he stood with his back to the fire and his feet planted on the hearthrug in orderly-room fashion.

Hew smiled feebly, as if he feared Mary would care little for such a ukase.

'Devil take this forthcoming ball!' he exclaimed suddenly. 'That fellow will be there, of course.'

' In his regimentals, too—a good old phrase that !' said Sir Piers. But the ball *is* somewhat of a nuisance, especially as Mary is not yet *disillusionné.* Yet she is not a child, that I may prevent her going to where she has set her heart upon. But one thing is certain ; she must neither speak to, nor dance with him on that occasion.'

' I should think not !' said Hew, savagely.

' It is very unfortunate for you, my dear lad, if she has conceived any absurd fancy for this young man.'

' Oh, I don't care much for that, or whether or not the bloom is quite wiped off the plum,' was the nonchalant ·reply of Hew, at whose remark the general elevated his eyebrows.

When Mary heard of this alleged conversation, of which Hew lost no time in acquainting her, though ignorant as to whether the matter in regard to poor Falconer was a deliberate fabrication of his rival or a coarse exaggeration, she only smiled scornfully at it, as ' a weak

invention of the enemy;' but her conviction was, that whether invention or not, it
was calculated to have a most fatal influence upon the already sweet relations
between herself and Cecil; and we can
but hope that its truth or falsity will be
discovered in the sequel.

CHAPTER II.

CECIL RECEIVES HIS CONGÉ.

SIR PIERS' indignation with Cecil Falconer for presuming to address his ward in the language of love was very great, and he was in the act of 'nursing his wrath to keep it warm,' and studying how to circumvent one whom he deemed only a well-accredited adventurer, when next afternoon the latter, all unaware of *how* the general had been schooled to view him, was ushered into the library, where the former was idling over the preceding evening's *War-Office Gazette*. 'It is easier to conceive than describe,' says Oliver Goldsmith, 'the complicated

sensations which are felt from the pain of
a recent injury and the pleasure of approaching vengeance.'   The two were
suddenly face to face !

But Sir Piers, a courteous soldier and
gentleman of the old school, though smart-
ing and indignant, was resolved, that whatever turn the conversation took, he neither
forgot their relative positions of host and
visitor, or as officers in her Majesty's
service.

He felt himself, however, on the horns of
a dilemma.   He had no precise right, he
thought, to act on Hew's painful information in any way, obtained, as it was, from
a source so subordinate ; and he could not,
without some distinct reason, forbid his
recently welcome guest to visit his house,
though he was resolved to tell old Tunley
to strike his name off the visitors' list.
Unaware of all the mischief that was
brewing, Falconer advanced cordially towards the old general, who rose and gave
him his hand, if not very frankly, and said,
stiffly :

'Captain Falconer, I congratulate you on your promotion, sir; I hope it will prove an incentive to future good conduct and *esprit de corps;* but avoid cards, sir— avoid cards !'

Ignorant of how the speaker viewed him as a gambler, almost an adventurer and man of obscure birth, all as alleged by Hew, Falconer was alike surprised by this pointed remark and rather indignant at the tone in which it was said, and the general bearing adopted by Sir Piers.

He now inquired for the ladies, and was snappishly told that ' they were well, sir— well ;' but whether at home or not, Sir Piers did not condescend to say ; so Falconer almost held his breath at every sound, expecting Mary to enter the room ; but he hoped in vain, for never even once did a light footstep or the rustle of a dress announce her vicinity. However, he had barely seated himself, when Sir Piers, as if reading his very thoughts, said bluntly :

' I wished to see you, sir, on a subject that has recently come to my knowledge.

You have been addressing Miss Montgomerie in terms which no honourable man would do, without the full permission of those who are nearest and dearest to her, and have thus her welfare and her future at heart.'

Falconer, who felt painfully that in tone, bearing, and expression of eye, Sir Piers was now very unlike the hearty and hospitable veteran who welcomed him to Eaglescraig, said, with a somewhat faltering voice :

'All who have the happiness to know Miss Montgomerie will ever have her welfare and happiness at heart, Sir Piers.'

'Am I right in asserting what I do, Captain Falconer?' asked the latter, ignoring his remark.

'Before being borne away by my feelings, and permitting myself to address your grand-niece——'

'And ward.   Yes, sir—well?'

'I ought, doubtless, to have obtained your sanction——'

'Or sought for it—well, sir—well?'

'And have satisfied you as to—as to——'

'Your means and position?' interrupted the old man, impatiently.

'Yes, Sir Piers,' said Falconer, taking up his hat, which he relinquished.

'By the way, it has never occurred to me to ask you fully and distinctly who you are—but now I seem to have some right to do so?' said Sir Piers, as all Hew's promptings came to memory.

'Who I am?' exclaimed Falconer, partially cresting up his head, yet colouring too evidently with mental pain, as the keen eyes of his questioner could see.

'Yes, sir.'

'I am, as you know, Captain Cecil Falconer, of the Cameronian regiment,' he replied, somewhat haughtily.

'Anything more?'

'In what way?'

'Family—antecedents. The devil! do you think that I would permit a nameless stranger to address Miss Montgomerie as you have done?'

'I am not rich, certainly—the reverse rather.'

'I don't care an *anna* for that, as we say in India; but as regards family——'

'Suffice it that I am utterly alone in the world,' interrupted Cecil, with a cadence in his voice that made the general feel some pity for him, though not inclined to yield an inch, for his words seemed to corroborate all that Hew had alleged or inferred. 'When my poor mother died, I seemed, for a time, to lose the last link that bound me to the world. To her I owe education, position, the commission I hold—everything!'

And now, when he spoke of his mother, his voice grew soft and infinitely tender, and a subdued light shone in his averted eyes—the light of love and a great reverence.

'And your father?' said the general, in a softer voice.

'I can remember but faintly: he died when I was very young. My mother never ceased to sorrow for him, and yet

I fear, at times, that her marriage had not been a happy one, or that he had not deserved one so brilliant and talented as she was.'

'Oho!' thought the general; 'this refers to the musical world, evidently. Hew is right, after all.'

'It was selfish of me, perhaps, to leave her to be a soldier, for she was alone in life; but it was inspired by love for her, and to gain her esteem, that I worked so hard to become worthy of her, and rise in all that might promote me in my profession. In the School of Musketry at Hythe, in signalling and telegraphy, at the School of Engineering in Chatham, I won first-class certificates, and laid them, like a happy school-boy, in her lap. Since then I have passed out, one of the first, from the Staff College; and if I went to India——'

'Ah yes; go to India, sir, that is the place!' said the general, soothed a little and almost forgetting the 'cards.' 'But our conversation has wandered from the subject that introduced it,' he resumed, 'pulling himself together,' and resolved to be cool and determined, and for Hew's sake to end for ever this love-affair. 'In addition to what I said, sir, I have to add, that an honourable man should not make advances to an heiress—I mean if he is poor—and, in my time, all the Cameronians were men of honour!'

Falconer thought that a Cameronian might still very well make love to a pretty girl with a long purse, ana not forfeit that commodity which the general so unpleasantly emphasised; but an emotion of hopelessness began to creep into his heart, and he rose from his seat, though reluctant to withdraw: yet the interview was fated to have an abrupt and harsh *finale*.

'Captain Falconer,' said Sir Piers, after a little pause, 'Miss Montgomerie has never disobeyed me since she came to my house an orphan; since she was a little child that stood upon my knee and nestled her face in my neck, begging me to tell her the same story over and over again—

often an Indian yarn of snakes, tigers, and what not—and I know that she won't disobey me now.'

'I hope not, Sir Piers, so far as I am concerned.'

'I am averse to long and vague engagements, and have made up my mind to terminate hers by a speedy marriage with her *fiancé*, Hew Montgomerie, my heir of entail, as you know. They must marry at once, or—or——'

'Or what, Sir Piers?' asked Falconer in a low voice.

'She loses every shilling of her fortune by marriage with another.'

'Gladly—oh, how gladly!—would I take her penniless; but I shall not be guilty of injustice towards her; she would be permitted to choose for herself. God help us!' said Falconer, in a very broken voice. 'Good Sir Piers, let me see her once again, I implore you, just for five minutes,' he added, scarcely aware of what he was saying.

'Better not, better not, sir; it is useless,'

said the general, growing stern ; ‘much
mischief may be done in five minutes.
Once and for ever, sir, let this folly end !
I brought you most unwisely to my house,
and you used your time there in seeking
to detach the affections of my ward, Miss
Montgomerie, from her affianced husband.
Of the good taste that inspired such a line
of secret conduct, I say nothing ; but I
repeat, that this scheme on your part (I
speak not of folly on hers, for I hope she
has been guilty of none) must end ; and I
have the honour to wish you—good-
morning.’

He rang the bell, and with a heart
swollen by many emotions, Falconer
bowed and quitted the room. As he did
so, there was in his face an expression of
painful humiliation mingled with reproach,
that powerfully brought back another and
an almost similar scene, when he had expelled from Eaglescraig his son Piers, and
when kindly old John Balderstone strove—
but in vain—to effect a reconciliation between them.

His cool dismissal by the general, and the curious questions of the latter, made Cecil's blood boil with indignation. Had he only known all, it might have proved a bad business for the bones of Mr. Hew Montgomerie.

Despite the injunction laid upon him, the moth could not be kept from the candle. A fortnight had passed since the general's ukase had gone forth, and yet almost daily, by accident, design, or tacit understanding, Cecil and Mary met, and had the joy of lingering in each other's society, and riveting still closer the links of love that bound them to each other, but not without a dread of being watched or discovered by Hew, whose favourite haunts, however, lay far apart from theirs.

The spacious gardens, the parks, the hills, the half-empty West-end squares and crescents, the picture-galleries and promenades, afforded many facilities for such, apparently unpremeditated, meetings as theirs, and to Mary it seemed as if she had

only now commenced to live, and as if all
her past life had only been leading up to
this, the end of which she, happily, could
not then foresee.

As for Cecil, the very demon of restless-
ness seemed to have taken possession of
him. Save when on duty, the Cameronians never saw him, and he was never
happy save when, if not with Mary, searching for her in those lounges where, in the
limited circle of the Modern Athens—the
City of Idlers—everyone is almost sure to
meet everybody else.

But he had one special annoyance to
contend with. All the regiment knew
that he had been the general's special guest
at Eaglescraig, and deemed it strange that
at all his dinners and dances given to them
now, *he* was never present. Why was
this? All deemed it 'deuced odd,' and
Cecil writhed under their surmises, some
of which were repeated to him by Leslie
Fotheringhame and Dick Freeport, and a
sentiment of defiance became engendered
in his mind.

And it was with fresh annoyance that on parade some morning, or at mess in the evening, he heard some heedless fellow extolling the rare beauty of the general's ward, and mingling the praises thereof with the extreme appreciation of his wines and the culinary efforts of his *chef;* and somewhat of a crisis was put upon this, when Sir Piers dined with the regiment, 'in full fig,' and wearing all his medals, on the anniversary of its embodiment, the 19th April, 1689, and treated Falconer with a coldness of bearing that was but too apparent to all; thus rousing a kind of resentment in his heart, and a greater inclination to defy him in the matter of his now secret engagement with Mary, for such it formally was : but then, how about the terrible power Sir Piers held over her in virtue of her father's eccentric will !

CHAPTER III.

IN THE PRINCES STREET GARDENS.

AMONG those invited to the house of Sir Piers Montgomerie was Leslie Fotheringhame, of course; but he knew, from Falconer, that Annabelle Erroll was still a guest of the family, as she and Mary were a pair of inseparables; and compunction for his past treatment of her, and doubt of how she remembered him now, with a great fear of being contemptuously ignored by her, led him to decline, on every occasion, the invitation accorded, on various pretences.

Annabelle Erroll knew of this, and was piqued accordingly, so the old breach between these two grew wider, if possible. Cecil and Mary, as 'a fellow feeling makes us wondrous kind,' had a great desire to make peace between them; the former had told her of the love-making and quarrel by the river, and her sympathy was readily enlisted in the matter.

'You do love him still!' said Mary, as the two were exchanging confidences in the seclusion of their mutual dressing-room at night; 'at least I know, by your changing colour whenever his name is mentioned, that you have not forgotten how to do so.'

'One cannot forget having loved—or having loved him; at least,' replied Annabelle, in a soft voice.

'Would you marry him if he asked you now?'

'Decidedly not!' exclaimed Annabelle, whose golden hair was floating over her snowy neck, while, unaided, she was plaiting it up with deft fingers and throwing it this way and that, in masses, turning her graceful head sideways to see how they fell, and perhaps to admire the charming curve of her own white shoulders.

'You do not believe me?' she said, as Mary laughed at her reply.

'No—because, as I said, at the very mention of his name, even by me, your cheek flushes and your voice trembles.'

'If they do, it is with just anger,' said Annabelle, 'and you are mistaken, dear Mary; and I have read, that when an estrangement begins between two who have loved each other, it is like a tiny stream of water, which goes on widening and deepening day by day, until it becomes a river no bridge can span.'

'Will I ever be estranged from Cecil?' thought Mary.. 'Oh no—no—no!'

Various pretty and amiable little schemes formed by Mary to bring them together, with Cecil's aid, failed, and yet their meeting ultimately came to pass in the most commonplace way imaginable.

With the opening season come the weekly promenades in the beautiful Princes Street Gardens, where the regimental bands play in the afternoons, for the delectation of the fashionables and idlers of the West End.

Bordered on one side by the most magnificent terrace and promenade in Europe, and on the other by the emerald-green bank of the Castle Hill, with all its waving trees, and by the mighty mass of the beetling rock on which stands the hoary fortress of a thousand memories, and more than a thousand years, these gardens are altogether unique; and already they were in almost their summer glory, for the air of the valley in which they lie was fragrant with the perfume of mignonette, of clove-carnations, roses, and heliotrope.

The carefully kept shrubberies were gay with borders of brilliant flowers, and amid this varied foliage the laburnum stood up in all the glory of green and gold. In swarms the happy children were gambolling and playing about on the velvet sward or chasing in zigzag fashion the bees and butterflies.

The fair promenaders were in all the

bright gaiety of their spring costumes, and the grand echoes of the castle rock were responding to the music of the band under our friend Herr von Humstrumm, when Falconer and Leslie Fotheringhame came sauntering through the throng arm-in-arm, the former watchful for the figure of Mary, and the latter languidly indifferent of all on whom he cast his critical eyes, in one of which a glass was fixed.

Suddenly Fotheringhame, who was rather a nonchalant personage, started, and the glass dropped from his eye, for, sooth to say, perhaps he could see better without it.

A young lady passed near him, with other two—an elder and a younger—unseen by Falconer, who was looking in an opposite direction; and there can be no doubt Fotheringhame looked after her with a yearning in his gaze, so sudden, passionate, and tender, as must have touched her heart had she seen it; but Annabelle Erroll, for it was she, was all unconscious of his presence. Her companions, we need scarcely say, were Mary Montgomerie and Mrs. Garth, an old lady who still dearly 'doated on the military.'

Fotheringhame's first inclination was to quit the promenade and effect an escape; his second thought was to stay, and see her once—only once again. And in sudden silence he continued to walk slowly to and fro with Falconer, till the abrupt turn of a narrow shrubberied avenue brought them both face to face with the three ladies, and there was no retreating; for as Hew disliked society of this kind, and was never present, Mary felt perfect confidence, and welcomed Cecil with one of her brightest smiles, while he—reading her wish at a glance—hastened to utilise the occasion by presenting 'his friend, Fotheringhame of Ours,' to Mrs. Garth and ' Miss Erroll.'

' In for it, by Jove !' muttered Fotheringhame under his heavy black moustache, as he lifted his hat, and saw before him, in her rare blonde beauty and magnificence of style, now fully developed by a few short years, the girl whose artless heart he had

won only to cast it at her feet—unclaimed
—unprized !

Mary's bright little face was dimpling
and rippling all over with pleasure, triumph
and exultation—all the more so, when she
saw that Leslie Fotheringhame was a man
of whom any woman might be proud, more
than ordinarily handsome, with an unmistakable tone, air, and bearing, that doubtless came of his early Lancer training ; and
now they were all conversing together with
apparent ease ; for although Mrs. Garth
knew what the wishes and orders of Sir
Piers were regarding Mary and Cecil Falconer, she did not conceive that they ex-
tended to the precluding of recognition in
a public place..

But had even the suspicious Hew been
there, not even he, on seeing the quiet and
respectful way in which Cecil raised his hat
and lightly took the gloved hand of Mary,
could have detected that there was between
them the soft and sweet and inexpressible
charm and link of a secret understanding.
And indeed none who saw the apparently

cool composure with which she greeted him, and talked of the beauty of the weather, the serenity of the sky, of the music then being discoursed by his regimental band, could have suspected that but an hour or so before, in a shady and sequestered place elsewhere, he had showered kisses on her lips, and hair, and eyes, and pressed her to his breast, '*à la* Huguenot,' again and again.

If deceit were practised in all this, it was not their fault, but was born of the pressure that was put upon them.

As the pair now began to promenade together, Cecil of course absorbed Mary, whom Mrs. Garth could not leave ; it thus became a matter of course that Annabelle fell to the lot of Fotheringhame, more than perhaps her proud heart assented to. His manner was careful, studied, and deeply courteous. She could not, as yet, detect the slightest sadness in his glance or tone, or aught of tenderness or reproach either, so well did he veil his manner, and yet his heart was full of her ; and thus these two,

who had been so much to each other—all
the world once—were meeting and acting
just as those do who have known each
other for half an hour, or less.

So they walked slowly on and on, all
unaware apparently that they were instinctively seeking the quiet and lonely avenues
of the garden, yet talking the merest commonplace all the while, though drinking
in each other's voices and tones, till the
groups of promenaders were all left far
behind, and the music of the band sounded
so faint and distant that the hum of the
honey-bees could be heard among the
flowers.

Then a silence—a long and awkward
pause occurred; they felt that platitudes
were failing them, and that they had a
lack of words—a lack that is said to prove
the deepest love, for where ' there is adoration there is paradise,' and Fotheringhame
began to feel much of the old adoration in
his heart for Annabelle.

' I have been on a long visit to Mary
Montgomerie, at Eaglescraig,' said the

latter, after a pause, during which she became very pale. 'She would insist upon me coming to Edinburgh with her; but the season here is nearly over, and I go back to mamma.'

'In Perthshire?'

'In Perthshire,' she repeated mechanically.

'Near where the silver birches overhang the Tay?' he asked with a caressing smile.

'Yes—and very soon,' said she, turning as if to retire.

'But not before our ball,' said he eagerly. 'You accepted our invitation?'

'Mary pressed me to do so,' she replied, colouring; 'and now we must hasten back to her and Mrs. Garth, for we are quite losing all that lovely music of Gounod's.'

'Stay one moment—do bear with me,' said he in an agitated voice.

'I do not understand,' she began falteringly, and then paused, yet looking him fully, firmly, and sadly in the eyes; 'have you aught to say to me?'

'So we meet again face to face, after all these changeful years, Annabelle!'

'I am simply Miss Erroll to you, Captain Fotheringhame.'

'I am only Lieutenant Fotheringhame now. If you remember the past——'

'Could I forget it?' she asked with sparkling eyes, while nervously twirling her parasol upon her shoulder, by its handle.

'Then pardon it, I pray you,' he urged in a voice which more than one woman had found it difficult to resist.

'Who is it that says, "Flowers and love have but a season"?' she asked with a little bitterness in her usually sweet tone.

'Annabelle!'

'I repeat to you, sir, that you must know me as Miss Erroll. I have been thoughtless in coming so far from my friends.'

'I am wrong in forcing my society upon you,' said he sadly; 'but that is a matter easily amended. In wronging you, as I did, dearest Annabelle, I wronged myself, and have suffered deeply accordingly.'

'Our meeting to-day has been—on both sides, unavoidable, Captain Fotheringhame. Let us return—if it is the best way to spare you further pain.'

She spoke very calmly and deliberately, yet it cost her a terrible and painful effort. She knew that she loved him still ; she felt even the eloquence of his silence, if such a term can be used, and now dared not lift her eyes to meet his gaze.

'Annabelle,' said he again, and took her hand in his ; then a quiver passed over her delicate form, but the proud girl accorded no other sign as yet of the power he still possessed over her. 'Do you despise me —do you hate me ?'

'Hate you — despise you ? — why use language so strong ? Oh no, no, Leslie, far from either — far from either !' she exclaimed, as if her heart would burst, and tears welled up in her dark blue eyes.

Then the artificial barrier himself had raised between them seemed to give way, and he told her in the tenderest and most earnest of words how fondly he loved her still.

'Let us not cast away the chance of reconciliation that God in His great kindness has accorded us, Annabelle,' he urged, pathetically; 'as I loved you first, I love you now—nay, a thousandfold more, for I have learned the value of the heart with which I so cruelly trifled; and now, I pray you—I beg of you to be my wife, Annabelle, my wife!'

She shook her head, and withdrew her hand.

'Is it to be thus?' he said sadly, but not reproachfully.

She made no reply, but kept her long lashes down and her soft eyes fixed on the gravelled path.

'Let us be now, as we were then, in the sweet summer days, when the silver birches cast their shadows on the Tay; and let us forget my folly, my wickedness—all that estranged me from your loving heart and divided us, Annabelle, when that fair and artful woman of the world, Blanche Gordon, cast her meshes about me.'

'And must I believe that you have loved me all these years, and love me still?' she asked softly, and with infinite tenderness of tone.

'God alone knows how tenderly, deeply and reproachfully, Annabelle!'

'But who knows how you might act if she came with her beauty and her meshes again?' asked Annabelle, who was smiling now.

'Do not be pitiless to me; and as for her — that woman — she is married, so, Annabelle——'

'Hush—we are interrupted!'

They suddenly found themselves environed by groups of idlers, and among others came Mrs. Garth, with Mary and Cecil, all of whom Leslie Fotheringhame would have wished very far away — at least on the cone of Arthur's Seat—at that precise moment.

Face to face again—at last, after all— after all — with Leslie Fotheringhame,

Annabelle was thinking; his smile, his voice and presence, were fast bringing back the old and seemingly buried, yet never forgotten love, to thrill her heart and every pulse as in the bygone time!

Her memory, her whole soul seemed to go back more vividly to those hours which neither he nor she had ever forgot, and now, whilst listening to his voice, she seemed to be out in the bright summer sunshine on the rippling waters of the glassy Tay, in his handsome boat with its crimson velvet cushions; she heard the plash of the sculls, the voices of the birds among the graceful silver birches; she saw the dragon-flies again whizz past, and the brown trout leap from the azure stream; and he too was in dreamland, and seemed to hear *her* voice; as when he first heard it singing:

> ' Love me always, love me ever,
>   Said a voice low, sad and sweet;
> Love me always, love me ever,
>   Memory will the words repeat.'

So they parted happily, these two, with

hopes to meet again, at least once, before the all-important night of the regimental ball, now close at hand.

That some mysterious change had come over the once nonchalant Leslie Fotheringhame, was soon apparent to the entire mess.

'What the dickens is up now?' said Dick Freeport to Falconer, on this subject; 'I am sure there is a woman in the case; and I am sure that fellow never had a love affair since he joined the regiment, or sought peril by imploring Maud to come into the garden.'

'All the cause of his being more hardly hit now, Dick,' said Falconer, laughing.

'If it is the case it will be a horrible pity!' said Freeport, as he shut his pet, and carefully-coloured meerschaum up in its crimsom velvet case with an angry snap. '"Of all the wonderful things, and there are many," says Sophocles in one of his choruses; "but none more wonderful than man."'

'Except woman, Dick, why didn't the old Athenian add,' said Cecil, laughing; 'so be assured there is a woman at the bottom of this change in Fotheringhame.'

'Shall we have her at the ball?'

'Most probably, so don't forget your magic ring with the blue stone, Dick; but you'll be hooked by a penniless girl some day, Dick!'

'A pity that will be, as manna does not fall from heaven now; but——the fact is,' continued the latter, still pursuing his surmises on the changed habits and bearing of Fotheringhame, 'that matrimony spoils a fellow for the service on one hand, and on the other, one can't think of bringing a tenderly - nurtured and high-bred lady into the meagre surroundings, and rough and round of barrack life.'

'Of course not, Dick,' replied Falconer; and yet—young though he was—he was not without his new day-dreams of a graceful and dove-like girl—of Mary Montgomerie—with tender smiling eyes and white hands, sitting opposite to him in that dingy barrack room, with its plain appurtenances.

But Mary was an heiress, and to wed and bring her there, would involve open war with her guardian, and too probably the loss of her inheritance!

'Would I had never seen her!' thought he; 'and yet—yet how vague and empty now would life be without her!'

CHAPTER IV.

PRIOR to all this, Sir Piers had taken poor little Mary seriously to task in person.

She was full of her own fond, happy thoughts, and in her own peculiar sanctum or boudoir, when the general, influenced no doubt by some recent remarks of Hew, came in looking black as a thunder-cloud —as black, at least, as he ever could find it in his brave old heart to be with her ; and here she was queen, for her boudoir was her pet place in the Edinburgh mansion.

The walls were silver-grey, picked out

with bouquets of roses. There were delicate cretonne hangings to match, and funny little black and gold chairs with crimson satin cushions; wood - brackets from Switzerland, and all manner of pretty china things, including porcelain pugs of all sorts and sizes; and here she received him with that charming, coaxing air, which no one could resist, and Sir Piers, perhaps, least of all.

She knew that a lecture was coming, and on what subject, too; thus she was a little nervous, and her pretty dimples came and went, so fast!

It never occurred to Sir Piers that there was gross selfishness in thus seeking to control Mary, and to absorb her fortune into the exchequer of the future baronets of Eaglescraig; though he certainly deemed that he was fully justified in preventing another family mesalliance, and with a nameless gamester.

'Give way to the whim of a girl!' he thought; 'no—no; I shall not be a chicken-hearted fool in my old age!'

'You have been out and abroad again, I understand, and without Mrs. Garth, Mary,' he began, while caressing her head, as she seated herself on a low stool by his side.

'I am close on twenty, and surely old enough to be trusted out of sight now!' said Mary, laughing.

'Hew says no — when that fellow is about.'

'Hew forgets himself!' said she, with a shrug of her pretty shoulders; 'I shall soon reach my twenty-first birthday, dearest grand-uncle, and surely then I shall be my own mistress,' she added, laughing.

To the general she had ever looked up in a sweet, grave, old-fashioned and child-like manner that gave him great power over her, but this he felt was, somehow, passing away. He felt some sympathy for her too, for the human heart is, perhaps, the only part of us that does not grow old with years; but he deemed that he had a duty to do, and heard her now with uneasiness, as he withdrew his hand from her head that nestled on his knee.

'Even in your twenty-first year, child, you will not be independent of me,' he said; 'I have still a control over your fortune, if I fail to control your future.'

'I care not for it!' said she, pouting.

'You know not what you possess, and therefore know not what you would lose; thus I am anxious—more than ever—to lose no time in transferring you and your heritage to the care of a husband I can trust.'

'Meaning the inevitable Hew!' she exclaimed, with a little angry laugh.

'Precisely, girl; I am proud to have an inheritor of our own blood, to my family honours, which, but for him, would pass away. If my poor Piers had only lived——'

'I would to Heaven he had!' sighed Mary, with all her heart.

'You tell me, Mary, that when of age you will be the mistress of your own actions. True. You never talked to me in this way before,' he continued, raising his voice and starting to his feet; 'but I tell you, that if you dare to countenance that fellow Falconer——'

'Oh, uncle, don't break my heart by talking thus!'

'Stuff! hearts don't break, though bones do. Let there be no clandestine correspondence, still less any meetings; but I trust to your honour, Mary—I trust to your honour, child.'

She blushed deeply, painfully, for she had an appointment with Cecil that very afternoon. She remained silent, and Sir Piers interpreted her silence his own way.

He knew that they must inevitably meet at the ball given by the regiment, and for himself to be at that especial ball was, he deemed, a duty he owed to the old corps; so, as for the chances of Mary and Falconer meeting, he would ensure that it would only be as strangers in a crowded ball-room.

'Yes, Mary,' he resumed, 'I trust to your

honour, that you will keep this fortune-hunter at a distance.'

'I do believe, uncle—nay, I am certain of it,' she said, in a pretty and coy, yet half-petulant manner, 'that Captain Falconer would marry me whether I had money or not. Oh how I wish I were without it!'

'Indeed!' said he with a cynical smile; 'for a commercial age, your ideas, my dear, are —to say the least of them—rather peculiar.'

'Now, you dear old pet, I wish you would say no more on this subject,' said Mary, glancing anxiously at a clock.'

'Why?'

'Because, grand-uncle, I don't want to marry anyone, and, any way, I will never commit the sin—for such it would be—of marrying one I do not, and never can love —there!'

'Meaning our Hew?'

'Yes, *your* Hew.'

'Don't be silly, Mary,' persisted the old man; 'you must and *shall* marry Hew, and there is an end of it!'

' But I have given my promise,' began Mary, feeling weary and desperate.

' Promise, to Captain Falconer ? The devil you have !   Did he dare exact one ?'

' Oh no, no.'

' How then ?'

' It came about somehow,' said Mary, as her fitful colour came and went.

' Did you promise—the devil, I'll explode !—to—to—marry him ?' asked the general with his back against the mantelpiece.

' No.'

' What the deuce then ?'

' To love him—and him only,' said Mary, piteously, softly, and in a low voice, ending in a little nervous laugh.

' And all this has come of my own folly at Eaglescraig ! damme, I'll—I'll—choke !' added the general, pale with anger, and feeling awkwardly conscious of the futility of it, with a genuine and honest fear of the future, through his unjust ideas of Cecil Falconer's character.

' Dear old grand-uncle, you have been

more than a father to me, ever since I was a tiny tot, just *so* high,' said Mary, holding a little white hand about six inches from the carpet ; ' and you must pardon me for all this—for Cecil does so love me,' she urged with tears, ' most tenderly and truly.'

' Folly—folly, all ! has life, has position, no other claim on you than that ? One born of such lineage as ours,' he continued, vaulting on his hobby-horse, ' requires to consider matters deeply. Disobey me, and I hand over your fortune to Hew ; it shall never be made ducks and drakes of by a gambler and adventurer ! By your father's will (how often am I to tell you this ?) it is absolutely in my power to disinherit you, if you wed without my consent.'

' A most cruel and illegal will !'

' Devised to save you from yourself, and with a strange prevision of that which was to come.'

' Unjust ! why should the dead be so loth to lose their grasp on, their power over, the living ?'

'Your father's great dread was fortune-hunters, lest you should be sought—as Falconer seeks you—for your money. Moreover, if this young fellow really loves you, child, he ought to think more of your happiness than daring to seek your hand.'

'Daring?'

'Yes, I say so, considering his origin! You are a romantic little goose! But girls in your position must not think of men in his.'

'Were you not a captain once?' asked Mary, softly.

'Yes, and a jolly ensign too; but then, as now, I was Piers Montgomerie of the Eaglescraig! My darling Mary, you are the apple of my old eye, and I should like to see you safe and sound under Hew's protection, ere the last bugle sounds for me, and summons me away to the Land of the Leal; Hew, save yourself, is the nearest to me in blood now that my Piers is gone, finding his grave I know not where—know not where!' he added in a broken voice, as he recalled the real or fancied, but terrible vision he had seen years ago, now. 'If money can bring happiness you and Hew should certainly have something very like it,' said he, returning to the charge.

'We should be very, very miserable—at least I should — with all our united wealth.'

'Tut, tut! how much more miserable would you be without it?' asked the general; 'and yet, sooth to say, pet Mary, I shall give you even to Hew grudgingly.'

'Why?' asked Mary, hopefully.

'Because,' said the old man, with great tenderness, drawing her head into his neck, 'then you will be for ever, not mine as you are now, little one, but another's! Where Hew goes, you will go; our old life will be gone; a new one will open to you, and I shall be a lonely, old, old man, lonely as when, years ago, I lost Piers!'

'But I am not yet married to Hew,' said Mary, kissing both his withered cheeks, from which the red tan of the Indian sun had long since vanished.

So there was a kind of loving armistice

between them for the present ; but all the general had said against Cecil increased Mary's loathing of Hew, a loathing that took the place of the toleration with which she had hitherto accepted, not his peculiar mode of courtship, but the mere fact of a residence with him in the same family circle.

And now, as she recalled all Hew's scandalous hints and rumours, she remembered the mutual impresssion which she and Annabelle shared at Eaglescraig, that by the expression of his face, the young subaltern Falconer *had* a history ; and yet she loved him not the less because, like Quentin in Scott's ' Ayrshire Tragedy,' he was :

> ' A young man, gentle-voiced and gentle-eyed,
> Like one whom all the world had frowned on.'

So the moment Mary was left to herself, she put on a thick Shetland veil, which very effectively concealed her lovely little face, and set forth in haste to hold a certain tryst ; thus the worthy old general's task had proved as yet a very fruitless one.

CHAPTER V.

THE REGIMENTAL BALL.

THERE is so close a family likeness among regimental balls in their general details, that we need scarcely describe that of the Cameronians, the chief importance of it to our story being the events that came of it.

All Edinburgh said it would be 'the ball of balls,' and beat those given a month before by the Dragoon Guards and Royal Archers. The officers were, of course, all dancing men, and there were few or no married ones to throw 'cold water' on the extravagances of the rest. It was held in the Music-hall and Assembly-room, two magnificent saloons connected by a stately vestibule, a place generally well patronised as a promenade between the dances. Each of these halls are about a hundred feet in length, and the first-named, on these occasions, is usually set apart for waltzes alone; here was the band of the regiment, in the lofty orchestra, under the guidance of Herr von Humstrumm, while a fashionable quadrille band was in the gallery of the Assembly-room, which has one of the finest floors in Europe.

A guard of honour, a hundred strong, under Captain Acharn, occupied the entrance to receive duly the commander-in-chief, Sir Piers, and other general officers; trophies of arms, shields, and claymores, the grouped banners of extinct Scottish regiments from the castle armoury, a double avenue of azaleas and myrtles, foliage and Chinese lanterns, with jets of perfumed water, spouting and sparkling in marble and alabaster basins, all testified to the good taste of Cecil Falconer and the ball-committee, who were there in 'full puff,' to receive the guests, who were now arriving as fast as the carriages could set them down at the east and west *portes-cochère.*

Yellow banners, with the trophies of the regiment, drooped over the staircases: 'Egypt' with the sphinx, 'Corunna,' 'China' with the fiery dragon, and lastly, 'Abyssinia'; and ever and anon the grand and inspiriting crashes of military music swept through the double halls. Kilted officers from the Highland depôt battalions, in various tartans; gentlemen in Highland dresses, Hussars and Lancers, made gay the scene. And the costumes of the ladies, the result of many an anxious consultation with mammas and *modistes* as to what would be prettiest and most effective, completed a scene in which a great amount of feminine loveliness and grace was not wanting.

In the vestibule, the young second lieutenants were flying hither and thither, supplying the ladies with enamelled programmes; the rooms were crowded by a glittering throng, and already the dancing had begun, when the voice of Acharn, calling the guard to attention, and the clatter of their rifles as they came to the 'present,' announced the arrival of Sir Piers and his party, and Falconer felt his heart give a responsive leap.

Roused and inspired by the music, the regimental trophies and familiar badges, and by all his congenial surroundings, the old general looked so bright and happy and he seemed to grow so young again that Hew, in his impatience to succeed him, might have thought that the Parcæ —if he ever heard of them, which is doubtful—were forgetting to shorten his span.

Smiling blandly on all, with all his medals and orders glittering on his gallant old breast, in full uniform, with sash and belt of gold, he moved through the brilliant throng, with Mary—Mary seeking for one face only—leaning on his arm; and he accorded even a pleasant bow to Cecil, as the latter hurried to his place in the dance with a tall and handsome girl, having arranged that Dick Freeport and Mary should be their *vis-à-vis*.

Once or twice as the night wore on, Mrs. Garth, from her place among the chaperons, detected a shadow cross the general's face, and knew that the sight of the familiar ' number,' the trophies and the uniforms, brought back to memory many a long-vanished face, and among them, doubtless, that of his only son.

Circumstanced as they were, Cecil felt all the mortifying absurdity of not putting his name even once on Mary's card, and permitting others to fill it—a rapid process; but there was a nameless sweetness in the conviction of the secret understanding that existed between them, and that she had specially implored him not to ask her. The general's alternate fits of kindness and severity, and his quick and impetuous temper, worried her. In his household he was absolute, or had all the desire to be so ; and thus with all her love and respect for him, a steady emotion of utter rebellion was gathering in Mary's heart ; and when she saw Cecil at the ball, she resolved that it would go hard with her if, by some little manœuvring, they did not achieve one dance together.

Yet her card was filled fast, as she had passed through the vestibule—the whole garrison fighting gallantly to get their names inscribed upon it — and she was overwhelmed with petitions for dances more than she could accord. All the subs had come to the ball prepared to fall in love with her; and, as Dick Freeport said, they were in duty bound to do so.

The dark dress of Mary—perhaps a curious one for a ball—black tulle, gracefully trimmed with ears of silver wheat, made the pure delicacy of her complexion, her white shoulders, round, polished and snowy arms, bare from above the dimpled elbow, all more startlingly fair. She had a complete suite of diamond and pearl ornaments. Even to her lover's eyes, she looked more than usually lovely; there was a tender flush on her soft cheeks, and purest pleasure sparkled in her soft face, as she swept round in the waltz with Fotheringhame, who was whispering to her of Cecil; and her lithe form seemed full of firm, yet delicate, strength and vigour.

. 'Beg pardon,' said Hew, who was no waltzer, but had ventured on one round dance with Annabelle Erroll, presuming on her good nature, and after canoning against several exasperated lancers and others, finally did so against Falconer; 'a gay scene,' he added breathlessly.

'Hope you will enjoy yourself,' was Cecil's commonplace reply to Hew, in whose eyes, even at that moment, he could read deep and defiant hostility, but partially veiled by a well-bred smile.

Remembering their gambling experiences, Acharn, a grim, dark officer, who had now dismissed the guard and taken his place among the dancers, would have opposed the invitation of Hew to the ball; but Falconer, loth to put a slight upon the general, and supposing that he had nothing personally to fear in his presence, enclosed a card to his would-be rival, and hence his appearance on the night in question.

He was disposed to be silent and sulky—silent in consequence of a total absence of ideas ; and sulky, because of Mary's too apparent happy preoccupation, and her succession of brilliant partners. Most—if not all—of the Cameronians were as good performers on a well-waxed floor as at anything else that is manly, and, as we have already hinted, the floor of the Edinburgh Assembly-room is simply the perfection of what that for a ball should be.

' What a cub that fellow Hew is !' said Fotheringhame to Cecil in passing, with Annabelle on his arm, her pale blue costume becoming her light blonde beauty well. ' Can it be possible,' he whispered to her, ' that such a girl as your friend can be capable of marrying one man while loving another—marrying this Hew Caddish Montgomerie while loving Cecil Falconer ?'

' I should hope not.'

' But women are such strange creatures !'

'Men are stranger still,' she retorted, with a bright smile ; 'but here comes our odious Hew—and I promised him this waltz.'

'He imposes on your good-nature ; bother the fellow !'

'Our dance, I think,' said Hew, lounging up.

' Number seven,' said Annabelle, affecting to consult her card, while Fotheringhame gave him an impatient stare, for his dislike of Hew was great.

'How handsome your cousin Miss Montgomerie is,' said he.

'She is full of goodness of heart and common sense too,' added Annabelle.

'I hope she will prove a girl of very *uncommon* sense,' said Fotheringhame.

'In what way ?' asked Hew.

'By preferring a Cameronian to any other man,' replied Fotheringhame with perfect coolness ; and Annabelle laughed to see the gleam that shot athwart the eyes of Hew, as he swept away with her into the dance, to begin a series of 'canons' again, and elicit remarks of wrath under many a moustache.

'I don't know what your plans are, old fellow,' said Fotheringhame to Cecil, as their eyes mutually followed Mary, admiringly, through the maze of waltzers, 'but, if I were in your place, I would write to Sir Piers, and give him fair warning that I meant to use every means to win his ward.'

'Nay, Leslie; I have already won her,' interrupted Falconer, a little triumphantly.

'Well—all the better; and if the girl loved me as she loves you, and as Annabelle tells me, I would have her in spite of all the guardians in Scotland!'

But there was no answering smile in the face of Cecil, who remembered how his last visit to the house of Sir Piers ended, and the summary manner in which the old man rang the bell to have him shown out !

And now for a time he remained among the crowd of men—the inert or uninterested —who hovered about the doorway, critically watching the dancers, and he heard Mary again and again praised, as she swept past in a succession of waltzes. The genuine praises of some delighted him; but there were occasional off-hand remarks that made him inclined to punch more than one head.

'Not a bad-looking girl at all,' lisped a Lancer; 'wish she wouldn't 'lay on the powder so freely, though.'

'Powder!' said Bickerton of that Ilk, a well-browned young fellow in the blue-and-gold-laced uniform of the Ayrshire Yeomanry, 'the devil a pinch of powder is there!'

'By Jove! to my mind, her dress is very *chic*. Regent Street couldn't turn out a better! Who the deuce is she?' asked another lounger.

'Oh! the daughter of Sir Piers Montgomerie,' replied some one whose information was vague; 'an old general officer— no end of money, and has refused no end of eligibles, and non-eligibles, alike.'

'Get me an introduction, won't you?'

'Well, perhaps—but her card has been full no doubt an hour ago.'

'Who is that swivel-eyed fellow that hangs about her ?'

'Her intended, people say—don't like the fellow; he once played me a fishy trick about a horse.'

'I have certainly seen a face like that girl's before,' resumed the Lancer, eyeing Mary through his glass.

'Perhaps—but you haven't seen many like it,' said Dick Freeport. 'I am lucky enough to have booked her for two waltzes.'

'Great success, this regimental hop of yours !'

Amid the painful doubts of his own position, his hopes and his fears, Cecil saw with pleasure how radiantly happy his friend Fotheringhàme and Annabelle Erroll were enjoying the ball and their own society to the fullest extent ; and sooth to say, though Blanche Gordon, the girl who had ' thrown him over,' was present, and looking very queenly in her costume and her loveliness, he seemed to have eyes only for Annabelle; and as his arm encircled her there was a depth of emotion in her tender blue eyes when their gaze met his, that called up many a loving thought, and, though they were silent, led both to remember the scenes of their past, upon the shining river, when the boat glided under the silver birches and the water-lilies floated by her side—scenes to be visited together, as they hoped, again.

But, as, if there could be no perfect brightness without a shadow, no perfect happiness without some alloy, it chanced that when seated together in the vestibule, for coolness, there occurred an event which —though Annabelle thought little, perhaps, of it then—she had bitter cause to remember afterwards.

A lady, closely veiled, passed quickly near them, after descending from the gallery usually occupied by servants and privileged spectators.

She dropped a card-case or purse, and Fotheringhame hastened to restore it to her, on which with a low voice, she thanked him by name, involuntarily as it would seem.

'Why are you here to-night?' he asked severely.

'To see—you.'

'How rash—how foolish—go home!'

She hurried away, and on Fothering-hame rejoining Annabelle, the latter could see that he had suddenly become very pale.

'Do you know that—person?' she asked while slowly fanning herself, and fixing her upturned eyes upon him.

'Why do you ask, dearest Bella?' said he, as if to gain time for thought.

'Because she seemed to know you, and called you Leslie.'

'Surely not; but so many people know me—the world is such a small place. I know her to be very unhappy, and this gay scene is the last place where I would expect to see her, even as a spectator.'

He spoke with perfect deliberation and confidence now, but failed to inspire his listener with the latter, as she read a sudden and settled gloom in his eyes.

The strange woman—a lady evidently—admitted that she had come hither to see *him*. Why? Then he had desired her to 'go home.' Where was her home? Who was she? And why did this chance meeting make him so *distrait*?

'Our dance now, darling,' he whispered, drawing her hand through his arm. 'One of Schubert's waltzes; old Humstrumm greatly affects Schubert,' he added with rather a sickly smile. But this little episode so, startled Annabelle, that the task of getting her fair face and soft complexion into 'society trim' again cost her an effort; and ere they could get among the waltzers in the Music-hall, a strange commotion there attracted the attention of both, as it did that of everyone; so the cause thereof deserves a chapter to itself, for Fotheringhame was struck with horror and dismay to see his friend Cecil Falconer borne past him to a retiring-room, reeling and almost senseless, in the arms of three officers of different regiments !

What had happened ?

CHAPTER VI.

HEW'S TRIUMPH.

PRIOR to this startling event, the reels, usually a great figure in such balls at Edinburgh, had been attracting the attention of Mary, who did not join in them; and the long line of more than a hundred dancers facing each other, presented a gay spectacle, from the number of uniforms, clan tartans, and occasionally the green uniform and great gold epaulettes of the Scottish body-guard, worn by some of the male performers.

The 'Cameronian Rant' was struck up by the orchestra in the Assembly-room, and old Mrs. Garth, who deemed herself quite as much a part of the Cameronians as the adjutant or the big-drum, and who had been vibrating, bubbling, and brimming over with pleasure all night, now felt her satisfaction culminate when the aged Sir Piers, with the courtly gallantry of the old school, led her forth as his partner, and looked round in vain for Hew and Mary, as a *vis-à-vis*, whose place was speedily supplied by Dick Freeport and a young lady whose interest he was exciting on the subject of his ring with the blue stone.

The reel over, the general had retreated breathlessly to his place, where he proceeded to button-hole the commander-in-chief—another old fogie like himself; and they were deep in reminiscences of the land of palms and punkahs, tigers and precious stones, when Cecil, discovering Mary with Annabelle and Fotheringhame in one of those flirtation nooks which are to be found in the corners of the Music-hall at such times, approached, and whispering that Hew had disappeared, and the general was busy, suggested that they might have one waltz together, as the double rooms always make a total confusion in the mutual engagements.

She murmured something, mechanically, about the heat of the room, the crowd, and so forth; his arm went round her; thrillingly her little hand returned the pressure of his own, having to the full as much effect upon him as any words she might have uttered; and in a moment they were lost amid the whirling crowd of hundreds of waltzers. Her great self-control nearly gave way in the delight of dancing with Cecil, 'under the temptation' which, as Wilkie Collins has it, 'no woman can resist —the temptation of touching the man she loves.'

Thus the soft pressure of the hand, which silently said so much, was mutually returned again and again, as Cecil guided her unerringly amid the mazy circles, till she paused, palpitating, blushing, and half-reclining, breathlessly on his shoulder.

'I have not had such a waltz to-night,

Cecil,' she whispered; 'so delightful, I mean.'

'Nor I, darling—one turn more!' And away they went again, but at a slower pace, which enabled them to converse at intervals.

They were not unseen, however, now, for Hew, who had been fraternising with one of the pretty waitresses who superintended the luxurious supper-tables in the wings of the hall, was watching them with a heart full of growing hatred of Falconer; he longed to do him a mischief of some kind—vaguely, savagely, and Mary too, for violating thus the express orders of her guardian. And how radiantly (disgustingly, he thought) happy they looked!

'I'll mar his wooing, and more!' muttered Hew, who possessed in an eminent degree that quality which is to be largely found in the least intellectual natures—low cunning.

As if she had some intuition of the *mal occhio* under which they were, she whispered:

'Hew has some deep scheme of mischief *in petto* against us—I am assured by quiet smiles I have read in his face to-night.'

'He is gone, I think.'

'I hope. so; he is so cruel, coarse, and unscrupulous—one, in short, to beware of.'

'Don't bother about Hew, darling; I fear more Sir Piers—and his never consenting.'

'I don't care for what Sir Piers says,' whispered the dear voice; 'I can never, never care for anyone but you, Cecil; I'll wait for you till I'm a hundred.'

At this cheerful prospect he pressed her little gloved hand again.

'I'm sure you'll wait as long as I—but oh, Cecil, I'm so wretched at times !'

But the bright *mignonne* face that smiled back to his didn't look wretched a bit, and in the glittering crowd at times, through which they were sweeping to the intoxicating crashes of the regimental band, while with each other thus, they felt as much alone as if the world contained no other couple than themselves.

'Is not love a thing worth living for, Mary, even for its own sake?'

- 'It is indeed, Cecil!' whispered Mary, with her brightest smile.

'A dream that comes, I am sure, truly and purely, but once in a lifetime.'

'And love, it is said, works miracles.'

'I wish it would work one with that dear old fogie, the general! When last he spoke to me it was somewhat like the stern parent in Allan-a-Dale, for he literally

'"Lifted the latch, and bade me begone."'

His arm was still encircling her; his left hand pressed her right; her cheek half sunk on his shoulder, their breath mingling as they swept on, intoxicated alike by the measure of the dance and the music of Strauss; in their souls unmindful of all ways and means—of marriage and the general; of houses; of equipages; of society and the world—unmindful of all, save that they loved each other, and were together alone—alone even in that brilliant throng, till Mary could spin no more; and

he led her well-nigh breathless to the most
sequestered seat he could find, between
two great vases of flowers near the cur-
tained gallery, under which some of the
supper-tables were, and his own (servant,
Tommy Atkins, who was in attendance
there, promptly brought them some iced
champagne.

On the third finger of her left hand,
Mary had a ring that Cecil had placed
there—a diamond cluster, and which she
was fond of drawing off her glove to contemplate, with a self-conscious aspect and
tender smile—a ring unnoticed by all save
Annabelle, who now wore a nearly precisely
similar emblem.

She had drawn off her glove now, and
as she sat fanning herself, while Cecil bent
over her chair whispering little nothings,
dear only to themselves, Hew Montgomerie,
unseen by both, came near.

We have told in our first volume that
Hew was a ' good hater'—one precisely after
the heart of the great Lexicographer—and
how he had made a vow to revenge himself

on Falconer—a vow all the deeper for being
an unuttered one; and the time to redeem
that vow had now come!

Hew's hand passed for a moment linger-
ingly over Cecil's goblet of champagne. A
close observer might have remarked that
Hew's hand suddenly opened and shut,
and that as he did so the wine frothed up
anew and curiously; but no close observer
was there, and Hew withdrew some paces,
and laughed his noiseless, joyless laugh, as
he watched Cecil, while replying smilingly
and fondly to some laughing remark of
Mary, put his hand to the goblet, lift it
from the table, and finish its contents at
a draught, like a heated and thirsty young
dancer as he was.

Hew then withdrew from their vicinity;
but all that followed, followed fast indeed!

Cecil became deadly pale, and an expression of agony came into his face. The
lights in the domed roof above, and the
figures of the whirling dancers below,
seemed to multiply *ad infinitum*; the music
sounded as if receding to a vast distance;

the four corners of the hall seemed to be
in swift pursuit of each other, as if it
revolved on an axis: he read a strange expression of utter dismay in the face and
dilated eyes of Mary, who had started
from her seat; he made a wild, but futile
clutch at the table to support himself,
while a half-stifled cry escaped him, and
he fell with a crash on the waxed floor,
when a crowd instantly gathered round
him, and voices in alarm rose on every side.

'Make way there—poor fellow taken
ill — the heat — the ventilation here is
horrible!' cried one.

'Stand back—stand back, please—air!'
said an officer of Lancers, authoritatively.

'Lift him up,' cried another; 'he has
fainted.'

'Screwed as an owl, you mean,' said a
voice there was no mistaking.

'Silence, sir!' exclaimed Captain Acharn,
sternly.

But Hew, with his cruel cold smile, and
an ill-suppressed gleam in his parti-coloured
eyes, thought,

'If there is any nonsense still in her head about this fellow, surely it must end for ever now!'

So Cecil, in a state of utter insensibility, was borne away by the hands of kind comrades, placed in a carriage, and conveyed home to his quarters by Acharn and Dick Freeport, who were in an intense state of concern and bewilderment; yet 'all went merry as a marriage bell' at the regimental ball, and the dancing continued till the morning sun began to redden the castle towers and Arthur's rocky cone; for hundreds in the rooms knew nothing of the matter; a few red-coats were suddenly missed—some engagements broken—and that was all.

Mary danced no more that night, of course—or for the remainder of the morning, rather—and all that passed seemed a horrible dream, in which, however, Hew, singular to say, bore no part as yet in her mind, notwithstanding the significance of her words of warning during the dance. No suspicion so utterly monstrous as the reality was likely to occur to a mind like hers.

The general and his party retired. He was horribly perplexed and shocked by an event so utterly out of his ken and experience, and he could recall no parallel case in all the long course of his military career—an officer taken *thus* in a ball-room ; for of course, such is human nature, that the worst construction was instantly put upon it.

'Hah!' muttered Hew, as the carriage bowled through the empty but magnificent streets to the westward ; 'this comes of taking too much cognac with his soda-water. He'll be drummed out of society, and the regiment too, I suppose, for this,' he added with a grin to Mrs. Garth, who sat back in a corner of the carriage and sobbed sorrowfully.

Finding that no answer was made to his ill-natured remarks, Hew said again :

'This Falconer, used to laugh at the colonel's jokes and toady to his betters ; but, by Jove, he won't have a chance of laughing at the colonel's jokes after this !'

'Silence, Hew,' said the general, grimly; 'but I am thinking more of the honour of the regiment than of him.'

'She will either marry me now quietly, or she will *not*,' thought Hew, triumphantly and pitilessly; 'if she does not, I suppose her tin will come to me anyhow, thanks to her father's will and this old fool, Sir Piers—shame to call the old fellow a fool, though, for being so deuced friendly to me!' he added mentally, with a hiccough.

It has been said truly, that there are times, which come into the lives of some of us, in which the agonies of years are compressed into a few minutes—yea, it may be a second.

And thus it was with Mary!

Annabelle Erroll had her own cause for secret unhappiness—the strange episode of the closely-veiled woman in the vestibule—but at present all her sympathies were absorbed in the great catastrophe of the ball, and the unavailing sorrow of her friend Mary.

CHAPTER VII.

THE mind of Cecil, next forenoon, when he partially awoke, and seemed to grope his way back to life and to the world, was a species of chaos. He was ill, sick, abed in the doctor's hands—too ill to think—too weak to rise. He found himself in his quarters in the castle, and the events of the past night confused themselves grotesquely and hideously with the prosaic features of the apartment in which he lay : the joy and rapture of his being with Mary, mingled with the remembered horror that seemed to envelop him, as darkness descended on his eyes and the ball-room whirled round him, and amid the circles of the dancers, the crash of the music and the murmur of many voices, he fell heavily on the floor, as all sense passed away, and he seemed to sink into a sea !

When he did begin to come round and rouse himself, he was sensible of a hum of voices, and considerable odour of vinegar and of cigars, in his huge room—for a large one it was ; and there were Acharn, Leslie Fotheringhame, and Dick Freeport and the doctor, refreshing themselves with brandy-and-water, talking about the ball and surmising about himself, sympathisingly, and in low tones.

'I cannot comprehend it,' he heard the doctor say ; 'a curious case, and not like imbibing too much. He must have eaten or drunk something poisonous at the supper-table. There was no sudden transition from heat to cold—he had undergone no great fatigue or excessive weakness to cause such a fit as overtook him ; but I have known strong and healthy persons, abounding in blood, seized with sudden faintings after violent exercise——'

'But, man alive, doctor, Falconer is one of the best round dancers in the regiment,' said Freeport.

'It must have been the closeness of the room,' said Acharn.

'It looks a deuced deal more like half-poisoning,' exclaimed the doctor, with a finger on Cecil's pulse. Then turning to Falconer's servant, Tommy Atkins, and a hospital orderly who were in attendance, he ordered his hands to be rubbed, and his head to be bathed with brandy, salts to be held to his nostrils, and a little wine, as soon as he could swallow it, to be given him—for he was unwilling to accept the idea that was forcing itself upon him, that Cecil had, perhaps, taken too much champagne over-night; and then he withdrew.

In defiance of the doctor's injunction, which was that he was to lie with a low pillow, Cecil struggled up into a sitting posture and looked rather wildly around him as he greeted his friends.

He felt that he was in a dreadful emergency—a coil—yet in his pale face there was that faint indication of a smile that is sadder by far than none; for he felt that however well-meaning and attached to him his brother officers were, they were certain to have but *one* fatal suspicion in the matter.

'What on earth has come to you, Falconer, old fellow?' said Fotheringhame. 'I never knew of your getting into a scrape like this, even when a greenhorn, who was fined a dozen of Moselle for first drawing his sword, or a ditto for the sergeants' mess on first carrying the colours!'

'By Jove! it knocks me into a cocked hat,' added Freeport; 'I can't reason over it—the whole thing seems so unnatural—so horribly unreal! This is a worse scrape than mine with the three daughters of the depôt commandant.'

'There was safety in the trio,' said Acharn.

'Yes—he couldn't marry them all, certainly,' said Fotheringhame, 'though I am not prepared to say that if the law of Scotland permitted it he might have tried to do so.'

'How *can* you fellows jest thus?' said Falconer, faintly.

'True—I beg your pardon,' replied Fotheringhame; 'but chaff and fun are such habits with us.'

'I fear that this affair will be no "fun" for me. Have I talked much nonsense, Dick?'

'Well—being screwed—Cecil, you certainly did talk a lot of stuff; but people do that at all times, and even when quite sober.'

Falconer felt his heart sink at the view his best friends were taking of this catastrophe. He felt that he was the victim of some hidden and mysterious circumstance over which he had no control; but how was that to be proved? and he knew that in the chief city of Mrs. Grundy the public always took the worst possible view of everything.

'You do not think—you dare not think,'

he exclaimed half-entreatingly and half-defiantly, 'that I forgot my position and the honour of the corps, and took too much wine last night—in uniform and at a public ball too, in presence of the general commanding and all the staff?'

'I fear, my dear Falconer,' said Fotheringhame, 'that it only looks too much like that very mistake.'

'By heavens! I was never near the supper-tables but once—and had but one glass of Moselle!' cried Falconer impetuously,

'But people will be sceptical in such matters,' said Acharn, pulling his long black moustache angrily; 'and from much of what I heard on parade this morning there is a devil of a row impending.'

'Over me?'

'Yes.'

At that moment there came a single knock smartly on the door, and the adjutant entered with an expression of grave concern on his face. After a few words of kind inquiry, and half apology, he said:

'I am so sorry for you, my poor fellow, but the chief is furious, and, by his order, I have come—for *your sword*.'

The words seemed to sink into Falconer's soul. He knew all this implied, and that, too probably, it was the beginning of his destruction—the beginning of a bitter end!'

So his sword was taken away, and he found himself under arrest—but arrest at large, as the adjutant informed him that he was at liberty to take exercise within defined limits, within the barracks, but not to go beyond the barrier-gates of the fortress, and not to quit his room otherwise than in uniform, minus a sword and sash.

All this was not new to him, of course, yet he had listened to the adjutant as one in a dream, and saw him take away the sword. After the departure of this important official—the grand vizier of the colonel—the gravity of the situation became painfully apparent to all, and it may well be supposed there was no more jest-ing then, and Falconer felt all the horror of the new position.

His mysterious illness seemed to grow worse now ; a dreadful ache racked his head ; his heart grew heavy as lead, and his spirit seemed to die under this disgrace and all it implied and all it imperilled, and as yet he had not the most remote idea that he was the victim of a wretch's revenge ; thus the well-meant efforts of his friends to rouse him and inspire him with the hope that he would yet get over it—that all would be explained—that all would be well in the end, and so forth, were made in vain.

Dick Freeport, Leslie Fotheringhame, and the entire corps were bewildered by the catastrophe, and poor Tommy Atkins, who doted on his master, was in despair— got very tipsy on the head of it, and had given him, therefore, three days in the black hole, to contemplate the unstability of human—and more especially of military —affairs.

Events followed each other fast now ;

and when again the adjutant most reluct-
antly visited him, it was to announce that
he was in orders for a general court-martial, and to furnish him, by the colonel's
instructions, with a copy of the charge
preferred against him, 'for conduct unbecoming an officer and a gentleman at the
ball,' together with a list of the witnesses
for the prosecution.

All the bright, youthful, and enthusiastic
hopes—the hopes cherished for years ; all
the visions of glory and honour conjured
up on the day he first donned his uniform,
were crushed and gone now, like the dear
love of yesterday, for the love of Mary
had—in one sense—come into his heart
but yesterday ; and yet, how strong and
keen, how tender and true it was !

So bewildered was poor Falconer by his
mysterious illness, the sudden giddiness
and unconsciousness in the ball-room, and
his symptoms since, that he actually began
to believe at last, or adopt the idea, based
perhaps on the remarks of his medical at-

tendant, that he had been guilty of what was unwillingly imputed to him.

And yet, how *could* it be ? Utterly unconscious as he was of Hew's vicinity to him on that occasion, the idea that he had been vulgarly, yea brutally, hocussed, never occurred to his simple mind, though the doctors hinted that he must have partaken of something deleterious.

Apart from his comrades of the mess, there was an intense interest in the regiment for Cecil; the soldiers, and even their wives, paid him surreptitious visits of condolence; and the children of his company, who had been the recipients of so many Christmas-boxes and bonbons, lingered with hushed voices under the windows of his room—the girls curtseying and the small boys coming to ‘attention’ and saluting him quite gravely as their fathers would have done; and Cecil felt all this keenly and gratefully.

In the barracks and guard-house, his affairs were under constant and serious consideration, through the medium of much birds'-eye, and among many stories of kindness and generosity, connected with Cecil's popularity among the Cameronians, was one which they recalled prominently now : how, on one occasion, after a long day's march of heat and thirst, far up country in India, when commanding an advanced picket before the position of a hill-tribe, he had found, on visiting his sentinels, one of them, Tommy Atkins, worn with toil, sound asleep—a crime which was death by the Articles of War, if reported.

But instead of making poor Tommy a prisoner with the quarter-guard, he had shouldered his musket and kept the post in person, watching over the sleeping soldier on the one hand and the hill-camp on the other, till the movement of armed tribesmen in front compelled him to fire and bring the picket under arms.

He saw less of his chief friend Leslie Fotheringhame than he might otherwise have done, for the time of the latter— despite anxiety for the affair of his friend

—was much occupied by Annabelle Erroll, and in dangling after her.

At last there came a day which Cecil never forgot, from the emotions of mortification and humiliation it occasioned him. It was a Thursday—the usual ‘march-out’ day for the regiment. From his window he watched its departure, with bayonets fixed and colours flying, in heavy marching order, and in all the pride and bravery of the service, while he remained behind a prisoner, disgraced, deprived of his sword and sash, with a terrible ordeal before him, and too probably a doom—to him—worse than death !

And he heard the drums grow fainter and fainter, till their last notes died away in the distance, and he heard only the beating of his heart, that followed them with painful yearning it had never known before.

Anon, when the regiment returned, Freeport told him that when passing the house of Sir Piers Montgomerie, it had been halted in column, when the fine old soldier came out on the balcony and was received with a general salute, which he beheld with swelling heart and glistening eyes, and then he attempted to make a speech, but his voice failed him—yet he made a short one—so short as only to be equalled by that of the Duke of Wellington to the Household Brigade, when, after keeping silence for some time, he said, ' Guards ! you know me, and I know you —stand at ease !'

' Was—was Miss Montgomerie on the balcony ?' asked Cecil, after a pause.

' No ; there was only old Mrs. Garth waving her handkerchief vigorously, and alternately mopping her eyes with it, poor old soul, as she thought, I have no doubt, of old John Garth of our Grenadiers.   I thought, it strange that the belle of our unlucky ball was not there.'

But Mary had been watching the regiment, sorrowfully, from her own room, and missing an absent face sorely indeed.

To her this was a time of great horror

and dismay ; each night that she laid her sweet face on the pillow, she thought :

' If I could only waken in the morning to find it all a dream—all a dream !'

But alas ! it was a dream from which there was no awakening. Blended with great pity and sorrow, she knew and felt now, in all its intensity, the love she had thought about, read about in romance, but never knew till she had met Cecil Falconer ; the love, that is, whether found or not, ever a young girl's day-dream.

To all, save Annabelle Erroll, she had to act the part of apparent unconsciousness of, or indifference to, all that was in progress. Abed, it seemed to her that she heard every hour struck by the adjacent clocks, and yet she must have slept a little, as the memory of more than one torturing or tantalising dream told her.

People, however, do get through everything somehow.

In the petty circle of Edinburgh society, the *malheur* of Falconer spread with many exaggerations, and with much rancour ; he

was a great bibber, a *vaurien*, and it was
not the first time, by many, that he had
been in such a scrape ; and there was much
lifting up of hands and eyes among the
self-righteous who abound in the northern
city of the Seven Hills.

Mary resolved to avoid hearing aught on
the subject of the nine days' wonder ; she
paid no idle visits, and was at home but to
few ; yet, as many of the few were connected with the service, the whole affair,
the court-martial, and what was certain to
come of it, were freely discussed in spite of
her.

And he had no one to console him ' up
there,' she would think, as she surveyed
resentfully the grand old fortress, with its
towers, turrets, and black portholes, which
seemed to her but as a great trap, or giant
lock, barring in Cecil from her and the
world. And all her good-natured friends
assured her, that the military trial could
only end in dismissal, ruin, and disgrace.
Would that she could go to him, and see
him once again, and assure him that what-

ever came to pass, she was his own still.

She was tearless and very quiet. She would not even retort upon Hew's bitter exultation over the affair—an exultation which his detestable nature rendered him incapable of concealing. Her sweet face looked blank and white, and nothing seemed to rouse her.

Kind old Mrs. Garth felt intense pity for her.

'Poor darling,' she would say, while caressing her; 'no tears yet—would that I could see you weep!'

'Why?'

'It would at least relieve your heart. You have yet to learn, dearest Mary, that with too many in this world the growth of love is unlike every other growth: it often expands and blooms strongest amid sorrow and gloom and the chill blasts of adversity.'

'I am afraid, Sir Piers,' said Mrs. Garth on one occasion, 'the girl is simply breaking her heart!'

'Simply breaking her fiddlestick!' growled the general, who was terribly worried by the whole situation; 'yet I should not be angry with poor little Mary,' he added in a gentler tone; 'God is very good! He took pity on me, a childless old man, and, seeing an empty corner in my heart, sent her to fill it.'

Mary could hear, incidentally, from time to time, the general in his pure dismay that a Cameronian should cause such *esclandre*, Mrs. Garth acting in his interests, even Annabelle in her sorrow, and not knowing very well what to think (as she had her doubts of mankind in general), all inferring by casual remarks that Falconer was quite unworthy of her— that she had made a lucky escape, and so forth; but they forgot that 'the woman never yet lived who could cast a true love out of her heart, because the object of it was unworthy of her, and that all she can do is to struggle against it in secret;' and poor Mary was no exception to the rest of her sex generally.

‘Look a little beyond the present, dear Mary,’ said Sir Piers, as he caressed her head, that nestled beside his knee, and passed his old shrivelled hand through her rich brown hair ; ‘I dare say you think Providence very short-sighted in sweeping out of our circle this interloper, who thought to come between Hew and yourself, a ne’er-do-well, an utter black sheep in birth and bearing !’ he added, angrily ; for in his rage at the probable slur cast on the regiment—*his* regiment—he was pitiless with regard to Cecil, who, for a time, had come between the wind and his nobility ; and Mary knew not exactly how Hew, artfully, insidiously, and openly, by turns, had succeeded in influencing Sir Piers against the victim of his own treachery, but she replied simply and firmly, as Cecil's love for her seemed something too sacred and too precious to be referred to so bluntly as it too often was :

‘Talk not to me of Hew ; had Cecil Falconer never been born, I never could have loved Hew Montgomerie !’

Hew was one of the many in this age of refined civilisation, who, though they have no fear of God, have a wholesome fear of the police ! Thus, with all his malevolent hatred of Falconer, he shrank from using a dagger or pistol, even secretly ; but he had resorted to a means of revenge more subtle and cruel than either.

The great military influence of Sir Piers might have arrested the tide of ruin that was setting in against Falconer, and might ultimately have been brought to bear upon the president and members of a court so honourable and impartial as a military one ; but Sir Piers was enraged by the whole affair, and his mind was so full of it that for a time he ceased even to prose about Central India. Thus, for many reasons patent to the reader, his influence, if used at all, was thrown into the opposite scale ; and so Falconer was left to his destiny, an inexorable one, by the *code militaire.*

'Surely it is sharp work, Sir Piers, resorting to a court-martial at once,' said

Fotheringhame on one occasion ; 'could not your influence with the general commanding——'

'Don't speak of it, sir,' said Sir Piers, testily, with a wave of his hand.

'Is there no other resort ?'

'None,' replied the other, sternly.

'Yet I have heard our lieutenant-colonel tell that when you, Sir Piers, were in his place at the head of the Cameronians, you were less severe on a similar occasion, but of more importance than a ball.'

'What was it ?'

'When Lieutenant Piers Montgomerie was placed under arrest.'

The old general blushed scarlet and then grew very pale. The occasion referred to was when the regiment was leaving Edinburgh for the East ; he had urged the men to behave soberly and with propriety during their last days in the castle, that all might parade and march forth in perfect order ; and nobly did they all respond to the appeal, all save one, his son, who came flushed from some late entertainment to

the parade in the early morning, to the
great dismay of Sir Piers. A court-martial
would have ruined his prospects for life ;
yet he was put under arrest, and, some ex-
ample being necessary, it appeared in
orders thus :

‘ Lieutenant Montgomerie, of the Grenadiers, will in future do duty with one of
the battalion companies.’

This was in the days before the Crimea,
when to be attached to a flank company
was equally advantageous and honourable.

‘ True, Mr. Fotheringhame ; the offender
was my own son Piers,’ said the general
with much emotion, yet more irritation at
the reminiscence ; ‘ but this affair of Captain Falconer took place in the face of the
city, as one may say ; so let the arrest and
charge take their course !’

How the drum for mess jarred on Cecil’s
ear when he heard it now ! Instead of
dining at that jovial table, and sharing in
the happiness of its social circle, he had his
solitary repast brought to him in covered

dishes on a salver, the repast he had neither the appetite nor zest to eat, and which he would rather not have seen nor faced, save for acting a part before his servant, Tom Atkins, a sympathetic fellow, however, who could not help thinking that had *he* been seen groggy in public, how much more easily he would have got over it than his luckless captain.

The sweetest and the saddest hours must pass away inexorably, and so the sad hours passed with Cecil Falconer.

Day follows day and night follows night —is not human life made up of these?—but nothing lasts for ever, thank God, was his thought, and the end, be it ever so bitter, comes at last. But bitter as those of Marah seemed now the waters of his life! He felt that Mary and he were parted for ever; that she could be his love no more, and that the day-dream of her could be dreamt over never again!

About this time he received a kind and earnest letter of condolence from old Mr. John Balderstone, who had conceived a

great friendship for him at Eaglescraig ;
but the terms of it served to irritate Cecil,
as they too plainly hinted, ' from what Mr.
Hew had reported, that on the night in
question he had been exhilarated a little
too much, perhaps.'

He tore and tossed it away with a
malediction; yet old John Balderstone
meant well and kindly.

Hew's satisfaction at the progress of
events was too great for concealment.

' Screwed as Bacchus at the regimental
ball !' he thought to himself; ' and this is
the cad who tried to take Mary and her
money away from me. By-and-by we'll
kiss and be friends, as the children say,
now that *he* is scratched for the running.
He'll be doing the " blighted being " style
of thing now,' he added aloud to Sir
Piers. ' How interesting !—it is quite an
idyll, whatever the devil that may be.
Or perhaps he'll be going on the boards
—back to the old trade of his mother
before him ! I have known more than one

broken-down army fellow who came out quite strong in genteel comedy.'

The general heard and eyed him sternly, but with silence. What would his emotions have been had he fully known *all?*

Hew, however, thinking it would be as well to be out of Edinburgh about this time, took his departure to the country, on pretence of a little fishing; and the eventful day of Falconer's life was close at hand.

On the night before it, to his own surprise, he slept the heavy, yet feverish sleep that follows great tribulation of mind and consequent exhaustion of power; yet not without a dream in which he heard the voice of the adjutant again saying gravely, and with commiseration:

'I have come for your sword.'

CHAPTER VIII.

ST. GILES'S clock, the castle clock, and on the dials of every other clock, the hands went inexorably round, and the day and the morning of the eventful crisis came inevitably at last, and Cecil put on his beloved full uniform, as his heart told him, perhaps for the last time—but minus his sword and sash !

He looked round his humbly furnished barrack-room, with the eye of one who was taking a long farewell of something, and a heavy sigh escaped his overcharged breast. Leslie Fotheringhame, who was to act as his legal friend in court, pressed his hand, and said in his off-hand way :

' Take courage, my dear friend. Keep up your pecker, old fellow; Marshal Ney's scrape was a worse one than yours.'

Through a crowd of idlers, witnesses and others, who thronged the ante-chambers and bare stone passages, they proceeded towards the mess-room, in which the court, composed of officers of the rank of captain and above it, was being con-stituted and sworn by the president, and all fully dressed in review order, with their swords and sashes, around a table littered with writing materials and a few volumes of military regulations.

The first incident that jarred on Cecil's nerves was the voice of the president, a cranky old Colonel, whose whole life had been passed in sinecure staff appointments, saying :

' Bring in the prisoner !'

And he found himself, after being intro-duced by Fotheringhame, with whom he sat apart at a writing-table, duly charged with 'conduct unbecoming the character of an officer, in having, on the —— day of ——, 18—,' etc., etc. ; to all of which he listened as one in a dream ; and still more did it all seem so as the day wore on. How bright the sunshine seemed outside, and how close and dark the ruin within that ill-omened room, which had been so often the scene of hospitality and convivial jollity.

Through the open windows came, as from a distance, the jangle of St. Giles's musical bells, with ' mingling din,' as Scott has it ; and their monotony and iteration galled his spirit, and from mere association of ideas he felt certain that he must loath them for ever after.

Of how much Hew Montgomerie was his evil genius, Cecil Falconer knew not, nor had the least suspicion. Yet he looked around the many faces in court more than once, expecting to see his parti-coloured eyes regarding him with exultation ; but that worthy was miles away from the spot. Among the spectators he saw many legal men, in black with white ties, who had come up from the Parliament House—that provincial 'gossip shop'—to stare, whisper, and make severe comments, which certainly were sometimes called for; and to draw somewhat invidious comparisons between the modes of administering civil and military law.

When the minds of those who compose any court, are fully made up as to the guilt of the prisoner, and know the sentence that must be passed in conformity to certain iron rules laid down by law and custom, the proceedings are usually summary enough, and so it was in the case of Cecil Falconer.

Doubt of his guilt or error there seemed to be none; most of those composing the court had been at the ball in question, and were more or less cognisant of the bewildering catastrophe; but all that Cecil and Leslie Fotheringhame, as his friend and adviser, desired to bring before the listeners, were the simple facts that he had just been dancing—that hence some strange giddiness might have come upon him in consequence; of the wine he had taken but a single glass, as they could easily prove; and they desired to argue these simple points earnestly, in the hope of modifying the opinion of the tribunal, and Fotheringhame wished to put a question to the lieutenant-colonel commanding, as ex-officio prosecutor.

'Stop, sir, please,' said a member of the court—Brevet-Major Rammer of the Royal Artillery, a fiery-eyed little man with grey spectacles and red nose—a man who had crammed at Woolwich, and was up to the ears in military law, though ignorant of all the principles thereof; ' this would seem to be a leading question, and, accord- to Hough on courts-martial, such questions cannot be allowed.'

On this subject there ensued much dif-ference of opinion, and Major Rammer made some notes thereon with a dry pen.

'Clear the court!' cried the president in consequence, and there was a general exodus of the audience.

'What utter stuff this is!' said Falconer to the adjutant, as they smoked a cigar outside, while the fourteen members of the court, the president and the deputy-judge advocate, seemed to be all speaking and wrangling at once; and after some twenty minutes' deliberation the court was re-opened, and all the audience trooped in again.

The question was voted 'irregular,' though neither Fotheringhame nor Falconer had stated what it was to have been: so, as the former was about to propose another:

'We are here, sir, to try Captain Falconer, not *you*,' said Major Rammer, snappishly; 'not you, sir, remember.'

'Of that circumstance I do not require to be reminded,' replied Fotheringhame, haughtily; 'yet I do not see why the prisoner, or I as his friend, may not question the prosecutor as to——'

' In Tylter, on court-martial and military law, in Hough and in Simmonds,' began Major Rammer, with emphatic solemnity, and glaring through his goggles round the table, ' it is distinctly laid down——'

' Clear the court !' cried some one else.

It was again cleared accordingly, and all the orderlies, idlers, and wondering advocates, had to make a stampede into the dreary stone passages outside.

The debate, whatever it was about, was a stormy one, and above the voices of all others was heard that of Major Rammer citing Hough and Simmonds. The president had never sat on a court-martial before—and, perhaps, had always hoped he might never do so, and never be called upon to give a casting vote in any question in this world ; thus he was induced to comply with the dictum of the fiery-nosed and irritable Major Rammer, in all matters in the present instance, and the charge was eventually brought clearly home.

The two doctors, though both fast

friends of Cecil's, when examined as to the after effects of his mysterious illness, only served to make matters worse ; and, as doctors proverbially disagree, they did so as to the symptoms on this.

'Clear the court!' once more thundered Major Rammer, and after it was cleared again, the major returned to the attack, flanked by Hough and Simmonds.

In short, the personage who alone could have thrown any clear light on the whole catastrophe, was utterly unthought of by all, and was enjoying himself in the country while waiting impatiently the result of his treachery as reported in the public prints.

When the defence came, the colonel, the adjutant, and others, bore the highest testimony to the goodness of Falconer's character and disposition, his attention to duty, the love borne him by his brother officers and soldiers, and his gallantry on more than one occasion in India.

Hart's Army List was not at hand as to the latter.

'Clear the court!' suggested Major Rammer, who required documentary proofs of the said 'gallantry,' though his own breast was bare of all decorations.

'Well!' exclaimed Fotheringhame, as they were again cooling their heels in the passage; 'if the proceedings of this day are published, they will read rather queerly;' to which he added something not meant for ears polite.

Why prolong this account—a painful legal farce, for such the ignorance of the president, and the interference of 'the well-read' Major Rammer made it?

To those who knew Cecil well, his handsome face seemed pale—a face always grave and dignified; and his eyes seemed to observe the proceedings with a strange listlessness.

As afternoon drew on Major Rammer offered less opposition; Cecil was allowed to ask a few questions, as the former perhaps found himself in a minority, though most industrious in distributing slips of paper, with observations and quoted 'precedents' all round the table. The tedious proceedings were at length closed—the opinion and finding given—the punishment, whatever it was, meted out, and proceedings on which the existence—certainly the future—of Cecil Falconer seemed to depend, were despatched to the Horse Guards by the swift night mail.

The weary Falconer's room that night was filled with sympathisers, and the proceedings were discussed, and 'that old pump Rammer' duly stigmatised, amid the consumption of much tobacco, champagne, brandy and seltzer, long after tattoo, the roll-calling, the last farewell sound of 'lights and fires out' had pealed from the citadel gate and in the Grand Parade, and after silence and the silver moonlight fell together on the vast fortress and its rock.

'I thank all much, very much,' said Cecil with no small emotion; 'but it is no use you fellows talking: there is nothing for me now but to drift quietly away into the dark sea of ruin—it may be death !'

His lips were working convulsively as he spoke.

' Let the worst come to the worst, I'll bear it like a man, and drag out the remnant of my life (without *her*,' he thought) ' an adventurer, a beggar, an emigrant—a soldier in some foreign service, perhaps— what matters it how or when the bitter end may come ?   I'll not shoot myself anyhow—that were the deed of a sinner and coward !'

' For God's sake, Cecil, don't run on this way !   It's enough to make a fellow's heart bleed !' said Fotheringhame with much anxiety of manner.

' Who knows what becomes of those fellows who go to the dogs, or are driven there ?' he asked bitterly.

' Take heart, man—take heart,' urged Dick Freeport, patting him on the shoulder : ' you'll be, at worst, put at the bottom of the list of captains ; and you're not very far above that now.'

'No, no, Dick; I read dismissal in the faces of the President and that artillery fellow who was so infernally well up in Hough and Simmonds.'

CHAPTER IX.

A PAGE OF LIFE TURNED OVER.

THE Horse Guards did not seem in haste regarding Cecil's affair; some days passed on, and hope began to flicker up in the hearts of all—even the heart of Cecil—of all save Hew, we should say, as that worthy scanned the morning papers, for what he wished to see, in vain.

Evening was always an intolerable time to Cecil at this period—debarred the mess, and secluded in his room, where, left totally to himself, he was wont to indulge in those dreamy reveries that are engendered by a good cigar.

At six-and-twenty or so, it is indeed a dreary thing, when, as a writer says, 'much of life seems still before us, and a dark unfathomable future lies between us and the grave; when it is a bitter thing to sit alone and ponder on the days to come, and discover no bright spot in the darkness, discern no kind hand to beckon us forward.'

There was an evening which Cecil was fated to remember long, when amid other scenes, and when surrounded by much of peril and suffering.

It was the sunset of a lovely spring day. Beyond the ramparts of that great fortress, to look on which to every Scotsman must seem 'the phantasy of a thousand years comprised within a single moment,' the distant glories of [the departing sun threw forward in dark and rugged outline the wooded hills of Corstorphine, bathing in ruddy light the waters of the Forth, with its shores and isles seeming to substitute the hues of heaven for those of earth.

Lost in sad thoughts he sat by the

window of his lonely room, dreamily watching the evening haze tinted with gold by
the sinking sun, that already involved in
obscurity the lower portions of the city,
the gardens where of old the North Loch
lay, and out of which the castle rock, the
spires and fantastic masses, the pillared
buildings on the Mound, rose as from a sea,
the gathering obscurity, lending a strange
witchery to that wonderful view.

Cecil was then in one of his saddest
moments. In his hand was a tiny packet,
and gently and tenderly he fingered it, for
it contained the withered daisies culled
from his mother's grave; and his heart
grew very full as her image came vividly
to memory with all the idolatrous love she
had for him, her only son.

'Thank God she knows nothing of all
this shame and misery! Yet, who can
say—perhaps?' he muttered, and cast his
eyes upward for a moment.

An essayist tells us that 'memory is
the peculiar domain of the individual. In
going back in recollection to the scenes of

other years, he is drawing on the secret storehouse of his own unconsciousness, with which a stranger must not intermeddle.' So Cecil felt himself a child again, and into that storehouse he looked back to much of love and sorrow, to many struggles, anxieties, and triumphs, known to him and his mother only—his dead mother, of whom we may learn much more anon ; and now by the course of events believing that Mary Montgomerie was utterly lost to him, he, clung more than ever to the memory of his mother, for she had been all the world to him, as he to her.

'Could I expect that she would spend all the best years of her life waiting for a fellow who might never be able to marry her ?' he had said once to Fothering-hame.

'But, man alive !' responded the other : ' she is able to marry you.'

'Was, you may say ; we are separated now for ever.'

Times there were when Cecil thought he should go mad, as the whole situation in all its details of too probable ruin and disgrace, together with the certain loss of Mary, swept through his brain with painful and provoking iteration.

Could it be that he was the victim of some plot? Hew had been near him on that night, he had heard; but that was all. Had twenty nights or twenty years elapsed since that fatal ball? he sometimes thought, for most strange seemed the confusion of time and inversion of events.

So full was he of much and heavy thought, that he did not hear his door open, or was conscious of any one approaching, till a dog suddenly leaped upon him, thrusting its cold nose into his hand, and anon licked it with hot, flapping tongue—Snarley, as if conscious that his friend was in trouble, for Snarley it was, grovelling and abasing himself at his feet.

Tommy Atkins had ushered in three ladies and Fotheringhame, their escort.

'Mary!'

'Cecil!'

The two names on each tongue conveyed a world of tenderness, and tender was the light that shone in the eyes of each—tender and yearning too, as they held each other's hands, poor souls, and oblivious of those who stood by and tried to look unconscious, held their hands fast mutually, as if each had recovered some dear treasure, combined with heart and soul.

'You here, Mary!' exclaimed Falconer.

'Yes, Cecil, with Mrs. Garth and Anna-belle.'

'If the general knew that I had cha-peroned Mary here,' said Mrs. Garth, tremulously, as she pressed his hand, 'I should certainly be discarded, and find myself homeless in my old age.'

'I thank you, from my soul, Mrs. Garth!' exclaimed Cecil; 'after all the evil that has befallen me, is he still im-placable as ever?'

'As ever,' replied Mrs. Garth, while Mary only answered with her tears, but Snarley, in the exuberance of his joy, gambolled about among her skirts, as if a

lively young rat was hidden there; and
Fotheringhame, thinking that the lovers
had better be left to themselves, took
Falconer's powerful field-glass, threw open
the window at the end of his long room,
and invited Mrs. Garth and Annabelle to
discover, if they could, the outlines of Ben
Lomond, and the lights of Stirling twinkling out at thirty miles distance, thus
affording the two aching hearts a little
interchange of words and caresses.

There are few women in this world who
do not resolve firmly and act vigorously
when the tender interests of their hearts are
affected; thus Mary had somewhat stepped
out of her path, at all hazards, to see and
console in his affliction the man who loved
her, and whom, she had begun to fear, she
might never meet again.

What course events might take she
knew not, but she knew well that she had
been pitilessly told to expect the worst:
thus a great pity filled her soul, side by
side with her love for Cecil.

Cecil's heart was too full for utterance;

he could only whisper to her brokenly, and fold her closely to his breast, while in a soft and cooing voice, yet brokenly too, she assured him of her belief in his perfect innocence, and of her love which would never, never change or pass away but with her life; and a great calm seemed to come over the tortured heart of Cecil as he heard her, and told her again and again how kind, and sweet, and loving—and how merciful too—it was of her to come and tell him all this.

Mary had now her own thoughts of Hew as to the fatal event—suspicions, but they were vague, intangible; and even to Cecil she said nothing of them, nor meant to do so, till the worst came, though she knew not in what form to shape them.

No one among us knows the depth or intensity of the tenderness we have for anyone we love or value, till on the eve of losing them, perhaps for ever; and the great solemn dread that falls on the heart —even as the shadow of death. And Mary, by a deep and solemn presentiment, seemed

to feel this, when, after a protracted interview, during which the same broken-voiced
and loving assurances were reiterated again
and again, at Mrs. Garth's emphatic request she rose to leave Cecil.

Why should they be rent asunder? she
thought. She was rich and thus powerful,
on one hand; yet how helpless were both,
on the other!

'I thank you, Mrs. Garth,' said Cecil;
'bear with us a little, for our burden is a
heavy one.'

'It has been truly said, dear Captain
Falconer,' replied the old lady, senten-
tiously, yet softly, 'that we must bear the
burden of our lives, whatever it be, and
content us with whatever lot God is pleased
to accord us.'

'True; yet mine may prove a very hard
one. But Mary's face, and voice, and tears,
I hope will give me strength in the days
to come, if they bring greater evil to
me.'

'All love you,' said Mrs. Garth, kissing
him on the cheek.

And while pressing Mary's hand, Cecil replied by the quotation :

' " The love of all is but a small thing to the love of *one !*" '

Mary had been possessed by a crave to see and to comfort him, if possible ; hence the unexpected visit. Like balm poured upon a wound, it had comforted him, and assured him of her love unchanged whatever happened ; but save in that instance, nothing had come of the visit, and the future was as vague and uncertain as ever.

Cecil did not leave his room at the request of Fotheringhame, who had a wholesome or nervous dread of anything approaching a scene or situation, and yet he was soon to bear a part in one himself!

Clinging to Mrs. Garth, how Mary got out of the fortress she scarcely knew ; hurrying down the steep stone staircase, past the gun-batteries, on which the great-coated sentinels now trod to and fro, and then through the deep archway (where whilom the double portcullis hung), and

under the shadow of the stupendous Half
Moon Battery.

Neither, perhaps, did Annabelle Erroll,
for she had painful thoughts of her own—
bitter, jealous and fiery thoughts — all
unlike those of Mary, in whose heart there
gushed up a passion of love, sorrow and
pity, that filled with hot and blinding tears
the gentle eyes her close-drawn veil concealed.

They had not come in the carriage, but
by a common cab, and as Fotheringhame,
with great tenderness, was leading Annabelle to it, she saw—beyond a doubt—the
veiled woman of the ball passing *in* by the
barrier gate.

Beyond a little nervous start as she
passed them—a start felt probably by Annabelle, whose hand rested on the arm of
Fotheringhame. He gave no other sign of
that person's vicinity; but the sign was suffi-
cient to make Annabelle withdraw her hand
instantly, and receive his farewell adieux
with a brevity and coldness that rather
bewildered him.

But the voice of Leslie Fotheringhame came indistinctly to her ears—he seemed to be speaking a great way further off than that barrier gate, where the Cameronian sentinel stood, and she could see the great battery with its cannon and port-holes towering overhead, as through a dull and misty haze.

What did it all mean?

CHAPTER X.

GONE !

IT is said that ' there is nothing so difficult to believe as a certainty, till we have lived long enough to feel that it *is* a certainty, and not a delusion ;' but Cecil Falconer soon realised the fact of his ruin.

With much genuine commiseration of manner and great kindness of tone, the adjutant had acquainted him that he had been dismissed generally—not specifically —and that her Majesty had no further occasion for his services, and that the general order, thereanent, would be out in a day or two !

Cecil had boasted of the strength given to him by Mary's visit; yet, when the crash came, his strength and spirit alike gave way.

'My good name and my commission were all I possessed in the world, and I have lost both!' exclaimed Cecil to Fotheringhame, who grasped his hand impetuously; 'what will life be, henceforth, for me?'

Fotheringhame felt for him deeply, keenly, yet scarcely knew, from the depth of his own emotion, and the desperation of the crisis, what to say.

'Think of Mary Montgomerie,' he urged, after a pause.

'I do think of her, but to what end or purpose? She is further removed from me than ever. To marry her would be to deprive her of fortune and position—to place her at the mercy of the general and of Hew; and I—what have I to share with her but disgrace?'

His sun had set—his day of life was over—over at its dawn and flush! His heart failed at the hopeless and penniless prospect before him ; and the impossibility of having to reconstruct a whole life for the future on some new plan, and with other appliances—or die !

'My dear Fotheringhame, thanks for your sympathy,' said he ; 'but the sooner I am out of this place, the better now.'

' And whither do you mean to go ?'

'Heaven alone knows—I do not !' was the half-despairing response.

The news spread fast, and, apart from his brother-officers, the men of his company came by sections and scores to shake his hand and bid him farewell. All felt for him, loved him and sorrowed for him, and the dark dream seemed to be in progress still.   Could it all be real ?

The first preparation for departure was to take from his desk the withered daisies culled from his mother's grave, and place them in his breast. An intense longing was in his heart now to be gone—to go, go, go—anywhere !

'I am going away, Tom,' said he to

Atkins, who was hovering about him, and mechanically polishing the sword he would never draw again.

'Where to, sir?' asked Tom.

'I don't know where to—as yet—but I'm out of the regiment now.'

'Out of the regiment,' faltered Tom, as if it was an impossible event, even after all that had preceded it.

'Yes; I am, God help me, a broken man!'

There was a sob in Tom's throat, and he ventured to wring his master's hand.

'And you leave, sir——'

'As soon as I can, Tom. Take this note to the paymaster—I'll need all the money I can get.'

Tom saluted, took the note, but hurrying into his kitchen, in tremulous haste took a little packet from his knapsack and returned to place it in Cecil's hand.

'What is this?' asked the latter.

'Not much, sir. You'll excuse me, sir. I can't go away with you, but I may help you, at least.'

‘But what is this—money?’

‘Only a matter of ten pounds sent me
by mother, to make me comfortable a bit.
I am sorry it isn’t more, sir; but if you’ll
take it to help you, for poor Tommy Atkins’s
sake, he’ll be a proud man to-night. You’ve
been a kind master to me, sir, and—
and——’

But here the private soldier fairly broke
down, and wept outright, ‘bo-hooing’ like
a whipped urchin. Falconer was greatly
affected.

‘Thank you, my dear fellow—thank you;
but this can’t be,’ said he: and he had no
small difficulty in getting Atkins to keep
the proffered money.

‘Look here,’ said Acharn to a group
next morning in the mess-room, ‘Falconer
had only his pay, and this sentence is ruin
and beggary to him; ‘ I have here a cheque
for eight hundred at his service, and I
know that you fellows, and ever so many
more of the mess, will stump up. We must
do something to start him, somehow or

somewhere; but how or where is beyond me, for poor Cecil is a soldier, and nothing but a soldier.'

'But where the deuce is he?' asked Fotheringhame, who with Freeport came in with genuine anxiety expressed in their faces, to state that his rooms were empty; that he had left the fortress ere tattoo was beaten last night, and Atkins knew not where he was gone.

'He has got from old Blunt, the paymaster, the last money due to him,' Fotheringhame said; 'and he has nothing with him but a small portmanteau and a brace of revolver pistols. Everything else—his uniforms, and so forth—he has, by a note, left with me.'

'Where can he have gone?' said one.

'Oh, we'll trace him somehow,' said another.

But all attempts to trace him proved utterly unavailing.

So he had left the regiment, silently, quietly and alone, and of course, under the peculiar circumstances, without the fare-

well dinner given to a departing comrade—
left it without shaking the hand of anyone
formally—quitting the castle in the night,
unseen and unrecognised, taking only a few
clothes and his pistols.

'What does he mean to do with them?'
asked Freeport.

'Where *can* he have gone—what done
with himself?' were the general surmises,
while his sorrowing friends looked blankly
in each other's faces, and Fotheringhame
had a great yearning to see and talk with
Mary Montgomerie on the subject, and
was not without a lingering hope that she
might be able to throw some light on the
mystery that enveloped the disappearance
of Falconer; but in this matter he was
mistaken, for the days passed on and he
was heard of no more.

Evil tidings fly fast : thus on the very
night of Cecil's departure, through the
general, his household became aware of the
fate that had befallen the unfortunate.

Looking like a saint in her pure white

nightdress, Mary sat on the edge of her bed, weeping bitterly after Mrs. Garth had left her, and refusing all the earnest yet commonplace comfort that Annabelle Erroll strove to give her.

'Oh, what shall we do!' she exclaimed, wringing her slender hands, for in the word 'we' there was an affectionate sense of identifying *his* existence with her own; and in this action, as in every other, Annabelle could not help admiring a good deal of that elegance and grace which marked every movement, posture and gesture of Mary Montgomerie. 'What shall we do! Crushed, poor and ruined as he is, he is dearer to me than ever. Cecil—Cecil—come to me, Cecil!' she added hysterically, and hid her face in the bosom of Annabelle, who was weeping freely too, and no doubt thinking of the woman with the veil, as she said:

'How unfortunate we are, dearest Mary, to have both become involved with men whose lives are enveloped in some cruel or degrading mystery.'

'Oh, do not say so—so far as poor Cecil is concerned,' replied Mary, with something of indignation in her tone.

Next morning found her face to face at the breakfast-table with Hew, whose features wore their brightest expression, and who was rubbing his cold fishy hands with unconcealed exultation ; but Mary had got over her weeping now. She was very pale, and to all appearance heard unmoved the general reading in the morning papers the final details of Falconer's catastrophe —*fiasco,* as he called it—to Mrs. Garth, who was officiating at the urn. But Sir Piers laid aside the paper as soon as he perceived her. All could see her pallor, and an expression of irrepressible anguish about her delicate lips—the result of mental rather than physical suffering ; and in truth Mary had not slept all night.

A letter lay beside her cup—a letter brought by morning post. It was addressed in Cecil's handwriting. Sir Piers was eyeing her firmly and inquiringly as she took it up hastily and placed it unopened in the bosom of her dress; but the moment breakfast was over, she hurried away to her own room to peruse it, with tears that blurred the lines, and hands that shook tremulously.

It told her briefly that he was about to leave his native land for ever, but for where he knew not yet, and cared not; and the concluding words went straight to her affectionate heart:

'Farewell, Mary—farewell, my darling —mine no more! farewell for ever, now. All is over with me. We have both been rash in loving each other so tenderly, without the consent of Sir Piers, your guardian; but our rashness has ended roughly, cruelly, and sorrowfully, especially for me. I have dreamed a happy dream in loving and being beloved by you—a dream the recollection of which will brighten all that remains to me of life, in the desolate path that lies before me.'

And so he was gone, without trace, as Fotheringhame eventually told her.

Again and again she pressed that tremulously written letter to her lips, and murmured,

'My darling—my poor lost darling !—surely he will write to me, or his friend, again !'

But days passed on, and became weeks and months, and no letter or sign came.

The worst had now come to pass ; her vague suspicions of Hew's complicity in the affair were useless now, and Cecil seemed lost to her for ever.

'Now,' thought Sir Piers, with grim satisfaction, 'now that this unfortunate fellow Falconer is gone, he will forget Mary, and she will forget him, and, as a matter of course, Mary will return to her senses, and Hew's time will come.'

Perhaps Hew thought so too.

'When she sees him no more she will cease to grieve for him,' said Mrs. Garth, 'and this sore trouble will be lifted off our darling's heart in time—please God, in time.'

But the very mystery that involved

Cecil's departure added to the trouble and thought of the girl he left behind him.

A nervous agony of mind and a great terror fell upon Mary—a terror that with Cecil's hopeless and aimless departure, none knew for where, a long and dull life lay before her, without the society of him for whom she seemed only now to have begun to exist—he so winsome, manly, chivalrous, and all her own.

Through the long weary hours of the night she often lay dry-eyed and feverish, without a tear coming to relieve her overcharged heart, for she and Cecil seemed parted now and for ever, as surely as if death had done so. Wild, at times, was the longing to follow him—but *where?*

Would she ever throw her soft arms round him again, and feel his lip meet hers!

Then the warm bright morning of the early summer would come mockingly in, and the routine of life had to be dreamily gone through.

So these two were parted thus, without

having knowledge of each other, in sickness or health ; and without the hopeful joy of a happy meeting, or reunion at any time, to look forward to.

It is ' when we are left alone with the reality of an anguish that has hitherto been but a dread, there comes the darkness which, like that of Egypt, may be *felt.*' And such was the dark anguish that fell upon the heart of Mary now.

CHAPTER XI.

'THE INITIALS.'

IN the last chapter we have somewhat anticipated the progress
of time, for in the first few
weeks after the disappearance of Cecil
Falconer, certain disagreeables in the love
of Fotheringhame and Annabelle Erroll,
fortunately for Mary, served to attract her
attention and draw her from her own great
sorrow.

Fotheringhame was always a welcome
guest at the house of the general. To
Mary he seemed a link with the lost one,
and through him alone could she hope to
hear tidings that might come to any

member of the mess. To the general, whom
he viewed, so far as his friend Cecil Falconer was concerned, as a stupid, obstinate,
proud, and avaricious old man, he was
specially welcome, as the patient listener
to his prosy reminiscences of India, of
battles and marches, of pig - sticking,
shooting expeditions, and potting man-
eaters, all of which Fotheringhame heard
with respect and feigned interest, that he
might the more freely enjoy the society of
Annabelle, and of Mary, whom he really
loved for the affection she bore his lost
friend.

His engagement with Annabelle was no
secret now ; but if it was a source of joy
to him, to her it was not without painful
doubts and fears, for he seemed to have
some secret which she, as yet, failed to
probe.

That he and the lady she had twice
seen, had some hidden and intimate knowledge of each other, the words overheard
by Annabelle on the night of the ball
seemed fully to prove. Then there was

his undisguised emotion on seeing her pass
into the fortress on the night of the visit
to Falconer, an emotion that inflamed
anew the suspicion, jealousy, and natural
indignation of a proud and sensitive girl
like Annabelle.

What was this stranger doing there, she
thought, passing the sentinels unchal-
lenged, as if it was her use and wont?
whither was she going, if not to visit
Fotheringhame in his quarters? Who,
and what was she, and in what manner related to him? Whence this vulgar mys-
stery which had suddenly come into the
lives of her and her intended, after their
reconciliation and complete reunion had
given her so much of the purest joy?

It filled her with a nameless dread, and
as women, in joy as in sorrow, generally
seek the sympathy of each other, now in
her jealousy, pain, and mortification, it was
natural of Annabelle Erroll to confide in
her friend and gossip Mary, while, in gusts
of pride and anger, she sometimes failed to
appear when Fotheringhame came to visit

her, or received him with a coldness. that certainly seemed to excite in him pain, surprise, and pique.

Hew, who had some intuitive perception of all this, and who dearly loved mischief for its own sake, brought home exaggerated, and even false, statements of how and where he had met Fotheringhame with ladies generally, and especially with *one* lady in particular.

'Who she is no one knows, but she is always attired in the richest and most becoming of outdoor costumes.

'And seems a lady?'

'Undoubtedly, so far as air and bearing go.'

'Most strange, Hew!'

'Not strange at all, Mary, as the world goes,' said he, with a laugh.

'If you are sure of all this, Hew,' said Mary, 'it is a wrong, a great wrong, to Annabelle.'

'Stuff!' said he. 'Why, Ulysses loved Penelope very well, but that did not prevent him from being very jolly with

Calypso. But people are generally known by the company they frequent, and we all know *who* was his particular friend. What the devil can that fellow have done with himself? He is too poor for the wine trade, and must have turned digger at Ballarat, or a donkey-merchant in Texas.’

Mary gave him a glance of ineffable disdain, and turned away. She felt keenly for the anguish and wounded self-esteem of her friend! and she felt deeply mortified that the chosen friend of Cecil should be playing the present double part of Fotheringhame, for the general had seen him with this lady, and he could not be mistaken.

‘ And Cecil, where was he?’ she would whisper to herself for the thousandth time, as she drew forth a locket with some of his hair.

‘ It is so little to have of him, and yet so much that it reminds me of him all!’ she would say, kissing it tenderly, and re-tying the tiny ribbon that bound it; ‘ my darling Cecil—my own darling!’

Anon she would drop it softly into her bosom, and let it nestle there.

But soon some brief and important events brought about a kind of crisis in the affair of Annabelle and Fotheringhame.

After leaving the general's house one afternoon, it was found that he had dropped a note on the carpet, a note which he had apparently drawn forth with his handkerchief, and Annabelle picked it up. The envelope was addressed to him in a pretty and free feminine hand, and the top of the page began, 'My dear Leslie.' Neither of the girls read more, but instantly replaced it in the cover. Annabelle, as she grew ghastly pale, gazed with sparkling yet doubting eyes upon the note.

What did it all mean? What was to be done?

It bore a monogram in blue and gold, 'F. F.,' and there was a sweet yet subtle perfume about the note that, like the florid monogram, spoke surely of a female in the matter, and of a feminine taste too.'

'What *shall* we do?' asked Mary, in great perplexity.

'Enclose it, dear, in an envelope of yours, and post it to him,' said Annabelle. 'I do not wish to seem as if I knew aught of it.'

Bursting with natural curiosity, poor Annabelle no doubt was; yet she was too honourable and ladylike to pry into the matter, though, sooth to say, it so very nearly concerned herself.

'Perhaps it is only a note of invitation,' suggested Mary.

'Scarcely,' replied Annabelle, with difficulty restraining her tears; 'but I shall end this, Mary, by bringing my most protracted visit to a close, and go home to mamma, who has been urging me to do so.'

So the note was enclosed and despatched, and another came from Leslie Fotheringhame, thanking Mary for returning the former, adding that 'it was scarcely worth while doing so;' and when next they all met, the subject was ignored;

but there was a cloud over Annabelle's
face, for the memory of the note, in con-
nection with other matters, haunted and
tormented her. But he, in manner, was
calm, affectionate, and unchanged—the
same as usual.

' It cannot be from Blanche Gordon,' she
thought, though she certainly was at the
ball. This woman—F. F.—can it be possible
that she is some former flame of Leslie's,
with whom he has renewed his intimacy ?'

Her jealous fancies ran riot, and not
unnaturally.

Next day, Mary, when attended by a
groom, riding in a sequestered lane, between trees and hedgerows, came suddenly
upon Fotheringhame and the unknown,
walking slowly together hand in hand, in
a calm, apparently accustomed, and affectionate manner, that filled her with so
much grief and astonishment, that, wheel-
ing her horse in another direction, and
escaping them, as she hoped, unseen, she
dashed home at a gallop, and at once
sought her friend.

Without removing her habit or hat, she threw her arms round the neck of Annabelle, who, though used to her impulsiveness, was certainly startled.

'Dearie—my dearie,' she exclaimed, 'can you bear evil tidings?'

'That may depend upon what they are,' replied Annabelle, growing very pale in anticipation.

'Well,' said Mary, in a broken voice, while drawing her friend close in an embrace, 'you must teach yourself to—to forget Leslie Fotheringhame.'

'Not a difficult task, perhaps, as matters have been going,' was the bitter response; 'but why?'

'I have had ocular proof that he is trifling with you and your love, and that he has, I fear, a wife already—this "F. F." no doubt.'

'Married!' said Annabelle, in a breathless whisper, while the four walls of the room seemed to fly round her and the eyes of Mary, who was impetuously grasping at a conclusion, wore a strange expression

in which high indignation was blended
with the tenderest pity as she related
what she had just seen, and added :

'Oh, my darling, be calm ! I am so
sorry to tell you this—but, but—what can
we think ?'

'Ah ! why does he deceive me so
cruelly—why labour thus to break the
heart of one who loves him as I do ?'

'You must learn to think and speak in
the past tense now,' continued Mary,
whose tears fell fast, and she clasped her
friend to her own bosom caressingly.

'Married,' thought Annabelle, 'that
cannot be ; but he is perhaps about to
cast me off—play me false for another
again !'

Anger and scorn struggled with love
and sorrow in her heart; but her blue eyes
were dry and tearless.

'Had papa been alive, Leslie dared not
have treated me thus !' she exclaimed ;
'but he knows I have no protector now,
save a widowed mother. I wish that I
had not met him again, Mary, or that I

were dead—dead !' she exclaimed through her clenched teeth.

Mary, alarmed to see the storm she had raised, now attempted to soothe Annabelle.

'We may judge too rashly, after all, dearie,' she urged; 'it may be only one of those meaningless flirtations to which most young men—officers especially—are, it seems, addicted.'

'What right has he to engage in such, even if it be so ?'

'Cecil's friend could never be so base !' urged Mary again. 'Oh, let us cling to the hope that it is something that may yet be explained away.'

'It—what ?' asked Annabelle impetuously.

'This apparent mystery.'

But less gentle than Mary, who was apt to take refuge in tears, Annabelle said with outward calmness, though she felt only despair and exasperation : .

'I fear that he is totally without principle—false as the fell serpent that beguiled Eve !'

And when night came she was thankful to lay her weary head on the pillow, though she did so, not to sleep, but to long that she was again at home beside her mother, and to agonise herself with doubts and fears as to the issue of this affair, to which she was resolved there should be a climax, either verbally or by letter, on the morrow, when Fotheringhame was expected to luncheon.

But on the morrow matters took a new and more startling turn, ere time for luncheon came.

Mary, who had been idling over the morning papers, suddenly drew Annabelle aside, and said:

'Look at this advertisement. Can it be that the creature takes the initial of his second name—if not his name altogether?'

Annabelle read what the speaker's slender fingers indicated, and it ran thus:

'Will L. F. meet F. F. to-day in the N. G. at twelve o'clock?'

'This is evidently an appointment between these two—and in the National

Gallery !’ said Annabelle. ‘Oh, it is intolerable !’

‘I must confess that so far as the initials go, it looks as if such an event was on the *tapis*,’ said Mary.

‘But this mode of correspondence is surely beneath Fotheringhame ?’

‘Though not beneath her — it is *her* request.’

‘If married, she would not resort to this. I shall go to the Gallery, humiliating though the act may be.’

‘And I too,’ exclaimed Mary ; ‘let the carriage be countermanded—we were to have driven this morning, but we shall set out quietly on foot.’

Attired in dresses and hats of different style and colour from those they usually wore, and Shetland veils tied over their faces—than which there can be no more perfect masque—they set forth on this expedition, which was one of great pain to both, but more particularly to Annabelle.

It was a bright April forenoon, rain-drops still rested on the fresh green leaves,

and sparkled in the sunshine, early flowers
bloomed abundantly in the gardens, per-
fuming the air, and the young birds were
twittering in the trees.   Pure and bright,
it was a morning calculated to make anyone feel happy without knowing why; but
the hearts of both girls were sad, and
Mary sighed as she looked at the great
masses of the fortress, steeped in the
radiant sunshine, and thought of him who
was away, she knew not where.

The National Gallery, with its Ionic
porticoes, was soon reached by the way of
Princes Street, and they entered the
western range of saloons, which contain a
very valuable collection of paintings by
old masters and modern artists.   At that
early hour they were nearly empty.

Dreamily Annabelle looked at the
various objects of art around her—the
gigantic Ettys, the sweet proud bride of
the victor of Barrosa—the long-hidden
Gainsborough—the girl-wife of Grahame
of Lynedoch; and then her eye saw the
figure of one she recognised again—the

woman who had so evidently come between her and Fotheringhame — seated in a corner, apart from all, with her veil half-down, and her eyes fixed eagerly and expectantly on the entrance-door.

The two friends could see that she was perfectly ladylike in style and bearing, in pose and action, and that her costume, though plain and quiet in colour, was rich in material. Wrath and pride flamed up together in the heart of Annabelle, and while shrinking behind a group of sculpture, that she might observe without being seen, she said :

' It seems to me most unladylike, this mode of espionage, and truth to tell it is humiliating in the extreme; but I have neither father nor brother to protect me, Mary, and so I must protect myself.'

' Take courage, Annabelle—perhaps we may deceive ourselves, and—and—oh, good heavens! here he comes!' said Mary, with a kind of gasp in her voice, as Fotheringhame, in ' mufti '—a very accurate morning costume—came with his swinging military step through the long gallery, and raised his hat with a somewhat sad and certainly fond smile on his face, as the unknown threw up her veil and advanced to meet him. But leading her back to her seat, he bent over her, and a low and earnest conversation ensued between them, yet not so low but that some of it reached the overstrained ears of Annabelle.

'It was rash of you to put in that advertisement,' said he; 'and I saw it by the merest chance, as I never examine the business columns of any paper.'

'Rash? but, dearest Leslie, it is rasher still, circumstanced as I am, to visit the castle,' she replied in a sweetly modulated voice.

Her face was a very fine one; her eyes were golden hazel—a perilous kind of eye —'light hazel, the fickle colour,' says a writer, 'the most fickle eye that shines— the eye ever changing, ever seeking something new, ever wearying of what it hath, ever greedy of enjoyment in the present, ever ungrateful for the past and unmindful of the future.'

Such were the eyes of the handsome woman on whom the face of Fotheringhame was bent with tenderness, and what a beautifully moulded face his was, with its heavy, dark moustache, straight nose and well-defined eyebrows.

'If my husband,' she began.

'Don't talk of him, Fanny!' he interrupted, angrily.

'Oh, the wretch is married!' whispered Annabelle.

'And her name is Fanny,' added Mary.

'And so the lawyers have got your case in their hands, my poor Fanny?' said he.

'Yes—and when may I get it out of them again?'

'The devil alone knows—he is the great master in all matters legal.'

(Now what could this case be, thought the listeners; here was a fresh mystery— perhaps degradation.)

'To serve you, I sold my troop in the Lancers, and with the money——'

'I know, Leslie—I know all, dearest. I have suffered much since then.'

'Despite all that, how handsome you are still!' said he, tenderly and admiringly.

'I was handsome a few years ago, as you know well,' she replied with a sad, but coquettish smile; 'but why seek to flatter me now, dearest Leslie, you of all men?'

'There is a flatterer beyond us all, Fanny—your own mirror.'

She laughed at this, but there was undoubted sadness in her laugh.

'Intolerable!' muttered Annabelle, and unwilling to hear more of this mysterious conversation she withdrew in grief and dismay, followed by Mary, who knew not what to make or to think of the whole situation.

They had barely reached home when Fotheringhame came punctually to luncheon, wearing the same dress he had worn at the peculiar assignation, easy and frank in manner, with his usual smile of tenderness for Annabelle, who strove to hide the coldness of her manner and the ire of her spirit, but utterly failed to check the nervous quiver of her sensitive lip.

Mary, who had to act as hostess, and who had no personal interest in this matter, scarcely knew what to do, or how to comport herself, full as she was of disappointment and just indignation. The abstraction of her manner was apparent to Leslie Fotheringhame, who scored it down to Falconer's affair; and as Sir Piers, Mrs. Garth, and Hew were all absent, she was thankful for the attendance of Tunley on the trio; but the luncheon proceeded with indescribable slowness and oppressive silence—a silence broken only by strained and disjointed remarks.

At last the cold fowl, patés, etc., were discussed, and a move was made to the drawing-room, where Mary did not follow the pair of lovers, over whom she saw a stormy cloud was impending, and thought the sooner it burst the better for them both—for Annabelle most certainly—and Mary's tender heart seemed to bleed for the proud girl's humiliation.

'My dearest Belle,' said Fotheringhame, attempting to take her hands caressingly in his the moment they were alone, 'what is the matter to-day—why this gloom and coldness of manner to me? In what have I erred or offended you?'

He gazed at her appealingly and passionately; but she snatched her hands away, and drew herself haughtily up to her full height, while her proud white face only expressed much scorn and much grief too.

'You treated me once shamefully, Leslie,' she began.

'Let the dead past bury its dead,' said he, beseechingly; 'and now, dearest Annabelle——'

'How dare you speak to me thus again?' she asked, with half-averted face, and her blue eyes flashing with a kind of steel-like glitter.

'Thus—how?' he asked, in a bewildered

and rather indignant tone, as it seemed to her.

'In terms of love or regard!'

'What *do* you mean, Annabelle?' he asked, after a pause. 'Surely you have not permitted me to speak of love to you again—since that happy day in yonder gardens—or rather lured me into it, but to repel and cast me off, in revenge, for our quarrel in the foolish past time; beguiling me by your sweetness, but to fool me in the end?'

'I do not care *what* you think.'

'Good heaven! can it be that you do not love me, Annabelle—do not love me after all?'

'After all—all what, sir?'

'I hope, Annabelle,' said he, in the first faint tone of irritation she had ever heard from him, 'that after all this smoke, you have some fire to follow?'

'I do not understand you, Fothering-hame,' she replied, restraining her tears by a strong effort; 'but I fear that you are involved in something very dark and very dreadful. Who is Fanny—Fanny with the hazel eyes?' she demanded, passionately; 'Fanny, who is in the hands of the lawyers —who is so afraid of her husband, and for whom you sold your troop?'

Bewilderment first, and then anger, appeared in the proud face of Fotheringhame, who certainly seemed not to know what to think, and grew very pale. Then he smiled, sadly and bitterly, with something of anger making his lip quiver.

'Surely, Annabelle,' said he, slowly, as if to gain time to think, 'you, with your superior grace and beauty, assured position, and the indefinable charm you possess for all, and more than all for me, need fear no woman?'

'Jealousy is stronger than fear, and I am humiliated enough to be jealous. You have secret meetings with a woman to me unknown!' she exclaimed in a low, bitter and concentrated voice.

He grew still paler.

'You cannot deny it?' she added, imperiously.

'I do not—deny it,' he replied, sadly.

'On your honour, and ere all is over between us for ever, tell me who she is, though certainly it should matter little to me now.'

He paused, and, with a deep frown, began :

'If you are acting on information given by Mr. Hew Montgomerie——'

'I am not—I act on information gained by myself, and even thrust upon me; and here ends all between us,' she added, tearing off her engagement-ring, and thrusting it into his hand.

'Annabelle, I implore you to be patient, and reconsider this.'

'How dare you ask me to be patient, under such insult and wrong? Go, sir—I hate you—I never loved you—I leave you to this Fanny, whom we saw in her fitting place, among the domestics, on the night of the assembly—this matron of the period, whom I saw entering the castle, doubtless, to visit you—the Fanny with whom you have secret meetings and a secret correspondence—begone to her, and cross my path no more!'

And sweeping from the room like a tragedy queen, she left him.

'Did she but know *who* that woman is, would she speak of her thus?' said Leslie Fotheringhame, almost aloud, as he quitted the house with an emotion of deep distress, not unmixed with shame and anger.

He made two or three attempts to alter the decision that Annabelle Erroll had come to, of casting him off for ever. He called twice at the house of Sir Piers, but on both occasions was told that she was from home, and Mr. Tunley added, was preparing to leave town. He wrote her a tender and most passionate letter which might—nay, surely would—have explained all; but it was returned to him unopened; and heaven only knew the bitter ache it cost the heart of Annabelle to act thus firmly and decidedly, for, sooth to say, the love of Leslie Fotheringhame had become, as it were, a part of her own existence, interwoven with her daily life.

She knew that their engagement had become known to many, and the inevitable *exposé* and gossip that must follow its sudden ending, exasperated her justly ; and thus pride struggled with grief for mastery in her heart, as she brought her visit to the Montgomeries to a close, and departed for her own home.

From casual remarks, Mary could learn that none among the Cameronians had ever heard aught of Cecil since the night of his disappearance. The poor fellow had passed out of their ken completely. Mary's grief was all the deeper because it was secret, and as time passed, the grass seemed to be growing over the grave of all her hopes.

When Fotheringhame left the regiment on leave, she ceased to have expectation of ever hearing of Cecil in any way, even through Freeport or others ; and it gave her much of a shock to learn that the mysterious lady—she of the golden hazel eyes—had left Edinburgh too—at least, so Hew gleefully informed her.

And now Mary—though she omitted all mention of this circumstance in her many letters to Annabelle—knew not what to think of Leslie Fotheringhame, save, perhaps, the worst!

She was sick of Edinburgh and its new associations—the ruin of Falconer and the too apparent perfidy of his friend; but she regarded with equal dread and disgust a return to the general seclusion of Eaglescraig, and the persecution of Sir Piers and of Hew Montgomerie, and bitterly in her heart did she inveigh against the absurdity of her father's will.

CHAPTER XII.

EAGLESCRAIG — wood and wold, field, garden and lawn— was in all the glory of summer now, when June brought with it, as usual, the fragrance of the red and white hawthorn blossoms, the song of the nightingale and the coo of the cushat-dove; May that gave fresh greenness to the young corn on the upland slopes, and studded the grass on the dairy farms of Cunninghame with white daisies and golden buttercups; June that saw the old general clad in grey, whipping the cool dark pools of the Garnock or the Irvine with rod and line, and the skylark soaring high amid the silver clouds—the full-uddered cows standing knee-deep in the heavy pastures, and the bees warring among the velvet buds; but where was *he* with whom Mary would fain have looked upon Nature and her native scenery in their glory!

Eaglescraig in summer was rather unlike the Eaglescraig to which Cecil Falconer had come in stern winter to shoot over the covers; but Mary's heart could gather no brightness from the locality, which, though changed and more beautiful than in those days, was so full of his presence and associated with him: the lanes through which he had driven her pony-carriage when visiting the poor on missions of charity; the roads by which they had ridden to Kilwinning and elsewhere; the garden wherein they had so often lingered; the ancient dovecot on the lawn, and the grotto where—but why did she torture herself, in the superstition of the heart, by recalling all that was, but never could be again?

As that heart foreboded, she was not very
long at Eaglescraig before the old subject
of her marriage with Hew Montgomerie
was resumed by Sir Piers, who nearly
found an ally in Mrs. Garth, who came to
the conclusion that everyone loved their
first love, as a general rule, and married
their second or third; though she was
not without her fears that such a marriage
would not be conducive to Mary's welfare,
and knew well that too generally, in the
end, 'as the husband is, the wife is.'

With all the regard that Hew affected
to profess for Mary, it did not prevent him
from growling heavily over exchanging
Eaglescraig for Edinburgh, where yet, so
far as its gaieties were concerned, everything was yet, as the Americans say, 'in
full blast.'

'Here, in the quiet of the country,'
said Sir Piers, 'she will have time
to think over the escape she made
from that fellow Falconer; and time to
think over what she ought to do, Mrs.
Garth.'

Time to think ! Poor Mary had plenty
of that : time to ponder in long and oppressive hours, as she lingered by the dovecot with the pigeons fluttering round her ;
by the burn that flowed at the garden-
foot, with Mudie's last new novel half-cut
and wholly unread in her lap ; and, lost in
a day-dream, saw the bees seek the flowers
and the butterflies darting to and fro,
while wondering with all the intensity of
love and pity where *he* was, and what
doing, now !

Sir Piers did not precisely see his way
to acting like the stern parent or fiery
guardian of the melodrama ; but he thought
that the time was approaching when he
must do something to bend Mary to his
purpose, and compel or cajole her into the
acceptance of Hew, his heir of entail and
successor.

'You knew that—that young man but a
very short time, Mary,' said he one day in
reference to Falconer, and playfully pinch-
ing her chin.

'True,' she replied, with a sweet sad

smile; 'but it does not take years to learn to—love. Was it so with you, grand-uncle ?'

'No, by Jove! we were in cantonments at Simmerabad, and expecting the route every day, the route for Jubbulpore, when Lady Montgomerie and I were married, egad! at the drum-head, I may say.'

But as far as Hew's interests were concerned, a visit from Mr. John Balderstone one day gave Sir Piers much occasion to think over them—and pause.

A close correspondence with Annabelle Erroll was Mary's chief solace and support about this time; they had so much in common to commune about. Yet the name of Fotheringhame never once escaped the former, though he was mourning that a girl with such an amount of strength of character and so much loveliness had gone out of his life—for Annabelle was a wonderfully beautiful girl—beautiful with the charms of glittering golden hair, of slightness of form and white purity ; tall, slender and full of grace ; and though her heart was wrung by the memory of all she had passed through since the night of the Cameronian ball—that night on which she had been so happy—she thanked Heaven for the strength it gave her to cut the Gordian knot and quit the atmosphere of doubt, perplexity, degrading deception, and chaos in which she had latterly found herself in Edinburgh. 'No girl could be expected to undergo that sort of thing over and over again,' as she once wrote to Mary ; so well it was, she added, that she had with decision laid the future lines of her life and that of Fotheringhame, so far apart from each other.

Hew was smoking on the terrace one forenoon, deep in the study of his betting-book—a study that did seem a very pleasant one, if one might judge from the expression of his face—when he saw Mr. John Balderstone, the faithful and jolly old factor and friend of the family, coming ambling up the long avenue, top-booted, on his favourite old roadster, an easy-going bay, high in the forehead, round in the barrel,

and deep in the chest, as John averred,
'all that a roadster should be;' and he dismounted at the entrance door with the air
of a man who felt himself at home and
sure of a welcome.

'Now, what can this old buffer want?'
thought Hew, sulkily, as the rider threw
his reins to Pate Pastern, who took the
bay round to the stables; 'but he is always
coming here, whether wanted or not.'

'Good-morning, Mr. Balderstone,' he
added, but without offering his cold, damp
hand, which the visitor had never taken
since the insulting trick had been played
him with the pair of jack-spurs.

Between these two there was no open
war, but a species of armed truce: a veiled
dislike or species of civil suspicion. Mr.
Balderstone knew pretty well the secret
character of Hew, and cordially detested
him. Hew knew the great influence the
old factor possessed with Sir Piers, and
had mentally resolved that when he 'came
to his kingdom,' *i.e.* succeeded to the title
and estate of Eaglescraig, Mr. John Balder-

stone should receive his *congé*, and pretty quickly, too; and that old Tunley, and even Sandy Swanshott, the aged game-keeper, together with Mrs. Garth, would have marching - orders, also. But the general ' was so confoundedly hale—seemed as if he would never die !'

'Did I not see Miss Montgomerie on the terrace ?' said Mr. Balderstone, with a twinkle in his bright yet dark-grey eyes ; 'she need not avoid me—bless her !—eh, billing and cooing as usual, I suppose, Mr. Hew ?'

Hew muttered an ugly word under his red moustache, and said, coarsely :

' I'll make my innings now, I suppose, as I have the field to myself.'

' And no red-coated rivals—eh ?'

'Look here, Balderstone, I don't like chaff; but I can tell you that Sir Piers did me a deuced lot of mischief by bring-ing that fellow here from Dumbarton, and petting him, egad ! as if he had been his own son. He is a regular old fool, Sir Piers !'

'I can hear nothing said against him, Mr. Hew.'

'At all events, I may indulge in a few bitter thoughts of this base-born interloper, who has caused so much turmoil.'

'Base-born—how know you that he is so?'

'Bah! I heard all about him in Edinburgh.'

'Not all, surely?'

'Yes, as sure as I am the heir to Eaglescraig! What are you laughing at?' demanded Hew, who had been in Tunley's pantry, sharply.

'I do laugh, and heartily too; but pardon me,' said old John Balderstone, whose paunch, enfolded in a deep corduroy waistcoat, was actually shaking, while Hew, by some intuition of coming mischief, he knew not why, eyed him dubiously, even savagely.

'By the way, have you ever heard aught of that unfortunate young gentleman?' asked the factor.

'What young gentleman?' said Hew, sulkily.

'Captain Falconer.'

'Oh! the singing woman's son—dancer, or whatever she was—no; how should I hear of him?'

'A pity—he must be found.'

'Found—for what?' asked Hew, growing pale, as he recalled the event of the ball. 'You'll have to seek him where he has gone.'

'And where is that?'

'The husks and the swine-trough—or the devil.'

'How can you speak so pitilessly?'

'I don't owe him much, I think,' muttered Hew, with an imprecation.

'God knows all you owe him.'

'How—why—in what way?' thundered Hew.

'As reparation.'

'D——n the fellow, I never wronged him!' exclaimed Hew, growing paler than ever, while his shifty eyes wandered restlessly about, and fear seized him that

John Balderstone had discovered, he knew not what.

But on this day the latter took all Hew's insolence of manner with wonderful equanimity, while his rubicund face seemed to beam and ripple all over with good-nature, and his eyes were twinkling as if he had something *in petto* that greatly delighted him.

'Reparation,' growled Hew, scornfully; 'reparation for what?'

'Here comes the general; he will tell you all about it,' said the factor, as Sir Piers, in an old tweed suit, arrived from a morning's fishing, with rod in hand, a full basket, and a venerable wideawake hat, garnished all round with flies and catgut.

'Welcome, John; welcome, Balderstone! you have business with me? Step in-doors. A glass of sherry and a biscuit before luncheon—tiffin, as we say in India—and then we'll hear all about it.'

'Business to which Mr. Hew may as well listen, as it interests him very nearly,' said Mr. Balderstone, with a sudden gravity of demeanour that impressed the former unpleasantly, and filled his heart with the alarm of the guilty, and he was the first to assist himself to a glass of the sherry which Tunley placed on the dining-room table; 'and as what I have to relate is not without interest to our dear Miss Mary,' added Mr. Balderstone, 'I would wish her to be present too.'

'Now what the devil can all this be about?' thought Hew, in a cold perspiration, as he took another glass of sherry, and thought of the ball and the court-martial that came of it, while Mary seated herself near Sir Piers, with her heart beating quickly and unequally, and her white hands trembling at her Berlin-wool work.

'In this matter I must begin at the beginning, as we used to read in the old story-books,' said Mr. Balderstone, polishing his bald head with his handkerchief, and looking up at the ceiling as if he would draw inspiration therefrom.

'Begin at the beginning!—don't say that,' said Sir Piers.

'Why, general ?'

'Because it reminds me how a poor fellow of Ours used those very words when about to relate some secret to me, as he lay dying by the roadside, on the march to Malwah, and though he began at the beginning I never heard the end of his story; so we buried him beneath a palm-tree, in his cotton quilt, the only coffin we could afford him—poor old Sandy Freeport—the father of Dick who is in the Cameronians now; and I remember that John Garth read the funeral service over him by torchlight.   Now fire away, Balderstone.'

The latter gazed fondly and admiringly on Mary in all her delicate beauty, clad in a loosely made brown holland morning-dress, relieved only by the spotless white cuffs at the snowy wrists, and a simple collar of the same at her slender throat, and said :

'I have some strange tidings for you, Sir Piers—tidings which may seriously shock your nerves.'

'Never ! d—n it, John Balderstone,

speak out, sir!' said the baronet with irritation. 'Who the devil ever heard of an
old Cameronian with nerves! And these
tidings——'

'Concern your son—your only son Piers.'

'What of him—now?' asked the other
in a changed and rather broken voice.

'His fate—his story.'

'Piers is dead,' said the baronet hoarsely,
as he recalled the shadowy form—the dim,
yet distinct outline—he had seen on the
night of terror, so long ago.

'I know it,' said Mr. Balderstone, sadly;
'poor Piers—poor boy! for he was but a
boy when compared with your years and
mine now.'

'Well.'

'How Piers married the penniless
daughter of a struggling artist, and
was therefore expelled from this house
—yea, from this very room, you know,'
said John Balderstone, speaking very
slowly and deliberately, while the general's
wrinkled hands grasped the knobs of his
arm-chair, and he fixed his hollow yet

bright eyes firmly on the speaker's face;
'how his commission was sold, and the
money went, you know too; but there was
much more that you and I never knew,
and never shall know, till the long, long
day when all things will be known. Piers
became an artist, and died in sore penury
some years after quitting his father's
house.'

'Where?'

'In an obscure street of Rome; but he
left behind him a son—the son of the girl
he had married.'

'My grandson!'

'And heir.'

Hew fastened his glass in his eye—the
green one—and glared at John Balderstone, who said:

'I know nothing precisely, though I can
guess of months of penury and struggling
to keep the wolf from the door, Sir Piers;
but that such was the case I have little
doubt from what I have gleaned: of wan-
derings from town to town—the husband
trying to sell his pictures, and the wife to

get engagements as a concert-singer—for she was highly accomplished—to support her husband in his last illness, and maintain her little boy. Piers was found dead one night at his easel. Pride prevented the widow from applying to you; and though she felt how sweet and dear it was to have her child as a precious link between her and Piers, she bestowed upon it her own name, which was Cecilia Falconer, and as Falconer the boy grew to manhood. Now you know *who* I mean!'

Sir Piers was struck dumb, and continued to grasp the arms of his chair with nervous energy, while Hew felt himself grow pale, and hot, and cold; and to the memory of the startled Mary came back the episode of Annabelle's ' Birthday Book,' and the curious admission of Falconer that he had been named Cecil after his mother.

In fact they were all paralysed and absorbed by the strangeness of this revelation.

' The proofs of what I say were sent to

me, and thereby hangs another curious story,' continued John Balderstone. 'A woman of indomitable spirit and pride, this Cecilia Falconer (or Montgomerie) resolved that never in your lifetime, Sir Piers, would she seek your friendship or alliance, nor until your death make known the rank and claims of her son ; but she died suddenly and unexpectedly, and the secret of *who* her husband was died with her, so far as Cecil was concerned, for indeed he knows it not even unto this hour.'

'Then how the devil do you——' began Hew, impetuously; but Balderstone silenced him by a wave of his hand.

'Her great musical talents won her powerful and titled patrons, and through one of them she got her son a cadetship, and by a singular chance he was gazetted to the Cameronians, the regiment of his father and grandfather.'

' I believe the whole affair a d——d tarradiddle, from beginning to end !' exclaimed Hew, while a kind of gasp escaped the general.

'You have not yet heard the end,' said
John Balderstone with a quiet laugh, as
he drew from his breast-pocket a large
envelope or packet, soiled by the dust of
many years, and covered with old and
foreign postal marks and stamps. 'In
this envelope, addressed to me, as her
husband's friend, the widow, when her last
fatal illness came upon her, sent for safety
three papers: the marriage certificate of
herself and Piers, performed at Rome;
the certified register of the child's birth,
endorsed by herself and Piers, and the
register of the latter's death at Rome. But
the packet on which such interests depended
had fallen behind a bookcase in my office;
there it has lain for fifteen years, and I never
knew of its existence till yesterday. And
here is your son's writing, Sir Piers, which
I never expected to see again in this world,
and it comes to me like a message from the
dead,' added Balderstone, with a tremulous voice.

'From the dead, indeed!' added the
general, more tremulously still, as he took

the documents and strove to read them through glasses that became moist and dim.

On the back of the marriage-register was written in a feminine hand :

'*Nov.* 5.—He died to-night, speaking of his stern father and not of me who loved him so ! Oh Piers ! my husband, my husband ! how shall I live without you—live on alone in the long years to come, unless it is for our boy ! In losing you I lose my all. For me you gave up home, friends, fortune, rank and position—all the world for me—yet, oh my husband, all the wealth of my love was yours !'

The *date* corresponded with the general's dream or vision ! Could Piers' spirit have flashed home at the instant of his departure ? Can such things be, and may men see them and live ? thought he.

'My poor Piers ! my poor Piers !' he groaned. 'John Balderstone, none but God and myself can tell how I have suffered in my soul for my severity to him in the past time.'

And so the long years had gone, and others had come ; and behold this was all that had resulted from the old man's pride, petulance, and injustice.   His only son had died in penury and obscurity; that son's wife had despised even his vaunted name and had taken her own ; and now, their only son, the legal and lawful heir of Eagles-craig, a crushed and ruined creature like his father before him, had been driven forth into the world, in darkness and despair, too surely also to ruin and death !

Sir Piers sighed bitterly, and seemed utterly to forget the existence of Hew, to whom this new state of things came like a prolonged roll of thunder.   To the former it seemed as if the irrevocable past was throwing its shadow over his present and his future—a shadow deep as the grave ; nay, that past made the future, and its shadow was over him still !

This accounted for the expression of eye that Mrs. Garth had traced in Cecil ; and Sir Piers had now a perfect key to that which had so often perplexed him—a something that the voice, face, and manner of Cecil brought to memory out of the mists of the past, causing him much vague and mental exercise—the resemblance to his dead son ; clearly accounted for now, when too late—all too late, perhaps.

'Scratched—out of the race !' muttered Hew with an oath, as he slunk away, and betook him to brandy and seltzer in Tunley's pantry, while Mary, her lithe and slender form full of energy, her dark and eloquent eyes filled with joyous light, seemed all unlike the languid Mary of the past month or so, as Balderstone's narrative came to an end.

Could it all really be in earnest, and no dream ? Cecil was her cousin—her own cousin, and that lawful heir of Eaglescraig whom Sir Piers, by the powers of his father's will, desired she should marry, while Hew was scarcely even a cousin by Scottish reckoning—little more than a namesake to her ; but Cecil—Cecil, where was he ?

Here was an astounding discovery ; an absorbing topic from the discussion of which, although their minds were full of it, and overpowered by it, they were compelled to cease during dinner and other meals, in that jerky, half-and-half way in which people are wont to adopt when servants are present, though the interest of their whole souls may be concentrated in it for the time.

But menials are close and watchful observers, and it was soon pretty well known to Mr. Tunley and all in the servants' hall, the topic which engrossed those in the dining-room—that Mr. Hew was not heir to the general's title and estate; but some one else was—*who* they scarcely could define. So the matter was speculated upon, twisted and turned over, eliciting a score of different opinions; but to all it was apparent that Sir Piers was perplexed, was daily conferring with John Balderstone; that Miss Mary—'bless her,' said they all—was radiant with joy; and Mr. Hew, with whom none sympathised —as might be expected—wore a sullen, baffled, and exasperated look.

The tables had been turned with a vengeance; but Hew had one crumb of comfort: Cecil was gone, no one knew where, and might never be heard of again, in which case he—Hew—would resume his old place as heir of entail!

In his anxiety to discover the lost, and make some reparation to the dead, Sir Piers forgot all the dark colours in which Hew had painted Cecil, and felt with regard to his son that, as Dickens says, 'there is no remorse which is so deep as that which is unavailing; and if we would be spared its tortures, let us remember this in time!'

Mr. Balderstone suggested that they should advertise for the lost one; but poor Cecil was now where no advertisements would ever reach him.

CHAPTER XIII.

BY THE MORAVA.

SUNSET, red and glowing, in a lovely land where a long spur of the Balkan mountains overlooks the current of the Morava, and where fair fields of rice and maize, hemp and tobacco, cover the upland slopes, for it is early in September, and the days are of great heat still. The golden shafts or rays of the setting sun shot upward from the flank of the mountain range, and shed their ruddy gleam upon the shining river. Slowly sank the glorious sun, as if reluctant to quit the strange and terrible scenes it was leaving: on one side the camp and bivouac of an army, with its fires for cooking and scaring wild animals, its piles of baggage and arms, groups of soldiers in thousands; on the other, the awful *débris* of a newly-fought field, covered with killed and wounded men and horses, broken caissons and gun-carriages, drums and standards, pools of blood in which the flies were battening; and paler then grew the upturned faces of the dead, as the last segment of the sun disappeared, and the brightness it left behind began to deepen from gold and red to sombre violet in the plain, though light yet lingered on the mountain summits.

In the tents and around the fires, men spoke little of the artillery duel that had preluded the conflict, of whether the Servians had broken the armistice, or the Turks had done so by opening with their guns, and little even of the victory; for the soldiers fresh from it and flushed with triumph and carnage, Servians and Russians alike, spoke only of the gallant but nameless British volunteer who had saved the life of the general, the terrible old Tchernaieff, and that of his chief aide-de-camp, the gallant Count Michail Palenka, and who had been made a sub-lieutenant on the field, and decorated after it with the gold cross of the order called the Takovo of Servia, and welcomed back with shouts of,

'Dobro—dobro! Ghivo—ghivo! (Well done—long life); hourah!'

In one of the terrible charges of cavalry, led by himself, Tchernaieff had his horse killed under him by a cannon shot, but this volunteer had remounted him on his own, and also dragged Count Palenka out of the terrible *mêlée.*

The Turkish horse were led, not by a Pasha or other officer, but by a frantic dervish, wielding on high a long staff, furnished at the end with a shining brass knob, and shouting : ·

'Allah is here! Allah and the angels who fought at Bedr!'

The Servian Hussars and Lancers, with the Russian Dragoons, advanced to join

issue in the charge for a third time, not
sorry to exchange close quarters for a
desultory carbine-fire.   Both sides came
thundering on, the Lancers with their
spears in the rest, the Dragoons with
swords pointed to the front, and all with
their horses well in hand, till within a few
yards, when they let them go at racing
speed, and dashed with terrible force and
fury among the Turkish squadron.

Anon the Lancers, finding their weapons
useless at such close quarters, slung them,
and smote heavily on every side with their
keen bright swords.   Long and hard was
the fight, and for a time the mingling
masses were too closely wedged in some
places to use even their swords, and
grappled with each other, while the entangled chargers, enraged and frightened,
reared, plunged, struck out and brained or
trampled into gore the dead and wounded.

Here it was the volunteer saved the
general and his faithful aide-de-camp,
covering them as they struggled back,
faint and breathless, out of the *débris;*

thrusting with his lance till it snapped in two, and then hacking his way out with the sword ; and it was only after it was all over, and he came afoot out of the field, dazed in aspect, with teeth set, eyes dilated and glaring with the fierce fever of battle, and clutching a sword, the blade and hilt of which were literally covered with blood, that he fairly knew what he had done, and the burst seams of his uniform showed all how well he had plied his weapon that day.

Thirstily and gratefully he took a draught from a tin canteen of Negotin wine, which a passing sutler gave him.

Cecil Falconer, for the volunteer was he, though in that blood-stained foreign uniform few would have recognised the once fashionable Cameronian officer, was sorely changed in aspect. He was browner visaged, bearded to the eyes, yet his face was worn and lined, and his eyes seemed sunk and keen, with the wolfish expression worn by those of men who are daily facing peril and death.

As a volunteer, he wore the uniform of a private—a brown tunic faced with scarlet, crimson pantaloons, now covered with blood and mud, and a grey cloth cap, not unlike the Scottish glengarry. Fighting in a cause for which—and in that of a prince for whom—he cared nothing; fighting in battle as a weaker spirit might have betaken itself to alcohol to drown the past and give oblivion to the present, poor Cecil had found his way to Servia, and had that day done wonders, setting little store on the lives of those he fought against—the barbarous and brutal Turks—and certainly none whatever on his own life.

Refused a commission in the service by the Servian minister of war—for, by the influence of long conquest, there is much of the Ottoman in the character of the Servian people, who are fatalists, and as distrustful of all strangers as a John Bull of the last century—he had joined 'Tchernaieff's Own' as a volunteer trooper, and on that day by the Morava had won his commission, and the cross of the Takovo;

but what a mockery they were to him, and how little he cared about them!

Since joining in the humble and apparently hopeless capacity he had taken, he had undergone all the perils and miseries of the Servian campaign; had been compelled to consort, at times, with fierce and lawless comrades, who were most repugnant to his refined nature; he had been generous to all with his money, when he had any, which was not often now; he had nursed the wounded, buried the dead, and won golden opinions from all; he had groomed his own horse and the horses of others; had to hew wood, to cook coarse rations, when there were any to cook; slept on the bare earth in the rain and the storm, or sharing a *tente-d'abri* when one could be got, and sharing it with a comrade—some unsavoury and unwashed Servian trooper, whose vicinity was, in itself, a horror.

As most people know, but a very short time ago the Christians in Bosnia and elsewhere took arms against their oppressors, the Turks, who were unable to suppress the insurrection, and soon after the disturbance was intensified by a declaration of war against the Porte by Prince Milano Obrenovitch of Servia, who, by his army, was proclaimed King of Bosnia, and whose father, the alleged slayer of the famous Cerni Georges, began life as a cattle-driver, and first distinguished himself in battle so far back as 1807. Born in 1854, Prince Milano succeeded Michail III. (who was assassinated); and as the new war spread into Bulgaria, as we all know, it took the form of atrocities unparalleled in modern Europe, unless we except the Cromwellians at Wexford and the Williamites at Glencoe. The villages of the Christians were plundered and given to the flames; their male inhabitants slain without mercy, under nameless tortures; women and girls carried off to slavery. The dead lay heaped in the churches to which they had fled for shelter, and dogs and hungry kites tore their flesh as they lay unburied by the wayside.

And now it was within forty British

miles of that Bulgaria, where so much wild work was being done, that on the evening of the 28th of September, after Tchernaieff had crossed to the left bank of the Morava below Boboviste, and fought one of the greatest battles in the Servian war—a battle in which Prince Milan lost 3000 men, killed and wounded, while the Russians lost in proportion, and had sixty dead officers on the field—a battle in which the explosion of seven Turkish powder-caissons added to the horror and slaughter—that Cecil Falconer found himself warmly complimented, and again and again shaken by the hand, by old Tchernaieff, as the saviour of himself and his favourite aide-de-camp, Palenka.

'We shall never forget your services and your bravery this day!' said the latter—a pleasing and handsome man—in French.

'And your promotion, monsieur,' added the general, in the same language, 'will be my future care, either with the young King of Servia, or with our Father the

Emperor, if you choose to take service in Russia, as so many, of your countrymen, like Bruce, Wilson, Greig, and Ochterlony, have done, attaining fame and fortune.'

The offer was not an inviting one, but Cecil thanked the general for his gracious notice of his service, and for the rank and cross conferred upon him; and the former then rode off to his head-quarters, accompanied by Count Palenka.

He was a short, thick-set man, reserved and haughty in manner and bearing, and covered with Russian orders and medals, won in no petty wars. His eyes were small, the lids heavy; his nose was large; his complexion a ruddy bistre colour, and his hair and thick moustache were somewhat of a mouse-skin hue. Whether it was the occasion or not, we cannot say, but his face, figure, and voice dwelt long in Cecil's memory. And now, to obtain some of that food and other refreshmen⁺ of which he stood so much in need after ί. day of such terrible work, he joined a group of officers of his own corps, who were lounging on the grass near a fire, at which their servants were preparing a meal for them, and all made Cecil—the hero of the hour—most welcome, proffering him their flasks and cigar-cases.

Singular indeed was the group, and striking too, on which fell the fitful flashes of the adjacent watch-fire, for night had fallen, and the firmament overhead was full of brilliant stars.

German, French, Italian, Serb, and English could be heard, amid the group, chattered in turn, and sometimes all at once. Rich and picturesque in contour and colour were some of the uniforms, and they were worn by men of several nations who had come to serve the newly-proclaimed King of Servia and Bosnia. In the uniform of his infantry there was a Nassauer, who had won his laurels and his iron cross at the gates of Paris, in the war of 1871 ; Guebhard, a captain of Lancers, a man closely shaven save his moustache, with a silent manner, and most unpleasant expression of face ; a dark and handsome

Bohemian baron, armed with a quaint family sword of fabulous antiquity, now captain of a Bulgarian band, wearing a sheepskin cap, a richly broidered blue jacket, and loose trousers that had once been white, with pistols and yataghan in his girdle. There were a couple of Russian Lancers in red, and a Hussar in a sky-blue jacket, laced with yellow, who wore Crimean medals and had been lads, no doubt, when our troops went up the heights of the Alma, and were too politic, or too well-bred, to show the real hatred they secretly bore to all Britons; and in the Servian uniform, as captains, with three silver stars on their scarlet-faced brown tunics, were two ex-officers of our own Foot Guards, whom we shall call Stanley and Pelham, who—in search of a new sensation—had come out to see life (and death too) in Servia; there was an English ambulance doctor in the truly awful chimney-pot hat of civilisation; and though last, not least, the ubiquitous correspondent of a London paper, in a kind of uniform—

a frogged coat and forage-cap—with a revolver at his belt, and a case of writing materials slung over his shoulder, as jolly and as much at home with everyone as if he had first seen the world and been weaned in a Servian bivouac, and ready to join with hearty goodwill a few who struck up 'La Belle Serbe,' the national chant of the country, to an air of great antiquity.

A light or two in the distance indicated the locality of the rather meanly-built village of Boboviste; and ever and anon cries and shrieks on the night-wind indicated that of the battle-field, where the ambulance - parties, doctors and nurses, were at work among the wounded and dying—Christians and Moslems alike.

The ex-guardsmen were chatting gaily together, and it seemed like a leaf out of the book of his old life to Cecil as he listened to them.

'A regular wanderer's club this, by Jove!' said one, laughing; 'made up of all sorts. I little thought to find *you* here, Stanley.'

'As little did I expect to find you.'

'Well, I suppose, with us both, it has come of backing the wrong horse too often —the little villa and brougham at St. John's Wood — the brougham with its three-hundred-guinea horses, and all the rest of it.'

'Not with me,' said Stanley; 'I found myself riding sixteen stone, and wished to bring down the flesh somehow. Besides, I was never much of a home-bird.'

'No,' assented the other, expelling his cigar-smoke in long concentric circles; 'but there is a novelty in all this new work here, with a vengeance. Only think, Stanley, in London, a few hours hence, would find us at the opera, at a crush in Belgravia, or consecrating the time to billiards, to the joys of Bacchus, and the chaste salutes of Venus, by Jove!'

'A devil of a business that last Turkish charge was,' said Pelham; adding, in a low voice, 'I shouldn't have cared if that fellow Guebhard had been knocked on the head—well, unhorsed at least, to-day;

he is a cantankerous brute—bad form, very.'

Cecil looked at the officer of Lancers indicated, but knew not then that a time was coming when he would heartily share Pelham's wish.

'This is not your *baptême de feu*, I believe, even in Servia?' said the latter to him, suddenly.

'No—I have received that baptism before,' replied Cecil.

'Where?'

'In India.'

'Indeed! What regiment?'

Cecil remembered the mode of his leaving the beloved corps; he felt his cheek flush hotly, and, affecting not to hear the question, turned to the war-correspondent of the London daily, who was making notes for ulterior press purposes, and took from Cecil's own lips his modest details of the charge in which he saved the lives of General Tchernaieff and Count Palenka—all of which episode would doubtless appear in the illustrated papers from sketches 'made on the spot, by our own artist,' whose immediate whereabouts was Fleet Street.

'How those Montenegrins fought to-day!' exclaimed Pelham, after a pause; 'armed with their sharp yataghans they came on like a living flood, after delivering their musketry-fire, and then flinging away their firearms, fell on with their blades in the smoke, precisely as the Scottish Highlanders used to do of old.'

'We'll have to write home about all these things.'

Cecil smoked in silence, and thought what home had he, or to whom could he write save to one who dared not receive his letter!

Amid this easy kind of talk, ever and anon the cries of pain—long-drawn moans, ending in a half-scream—came on the breeze from the adjacent battle-field.

'We shall hear the howling of the evil *vilas* to-night,' said Guebhard, with a grim smile, as he took the meerschaum from his moustached mouth.

'Who are they?' asked Cecil, whose knowledge of Italian and German stood him in good stead amid the polyglot kind of conversation that went on around him.

'Don't you know?' said Guebhard, a little superciliously; 'but it is a Servian idea—superstition if you will—that spirits so named come at midnight to exult over the slain; these are the hideous and fiendish *vilas,* for there are others that are handsome and good.'

Coffee and cigarettes discussed, and a bottle or two of *vina* drunk to wash down mutton-chops fried in a flat earthen pot with a wooden handle, stuck into the hottest part of the bivouac fire, Cecil repaired to the place where his troop had picketed their horses, and looked after his own, which Tchernaieff had sent back to the bivouac. It was unbitted and munching some chopped forage; he relaxed the girths, and, rolled in his great coarse trooper's cloak, lay down on the bare earth beside it, though rain was beginning to fall. He was sore in every limb, and

weary with the events of the day. He was
without a wound, but many a buffet, blow,
and strain, got he knew not how, began to
make his bones ache now, as he thought
over the stirring events of the day, and
gave himself up—as he too often did—to
sad and harrowing reflections.

Mary and the Cameronians—the regiment and Mary! was it the past life or
the present one that was a dream? So
far away did the old life seem now, that
though some of the events we have related
happened but a few months since, years
seemed to have elapsed since Mary's last
love-kiss lingered on his lips on that
twilight evening in Edinburgh, and when
he listened for the last time to the sound
of her voice—the voice that had been for
a time, and was still, the music of his life.

Oblivious of the pouring rain and sodden
bivouac, he lay there thinking not of the
past battle, or the present glory now; he
was remembering the regimental ball—the
lights, the music, the swift tender expression of Mary's eyes as she swept through

the dance with him—their first and last
dance, the returned pressure of her soft
hand, the touch of her hair on his cheek;
all the exultation of the time, and more
than all, her secret visit to him in the old
grey fortress of the city!

Could she but see him now!

His hopes—if he had any—his plans and
desires, the scenes around him, his companions and his circumstances, were all
changed now, as thoroughly as if he had
been born in a new, or other age. The
world rushes past so fast now (for steam
destroys time and distance), that his troubles
were beginning to seem old; or as if the
whole of his former life had passed away,
and that if he was to cut out fortune, fame,
and at least food, in the new one, the old
life could not be forgotten too soon.

But Mary Montgomerie was the central
figure in that former world still.

'How completely the romance has died
out of my life!' he thought; 'and our love,
it seems so like a dream to me now—but a
sweet and beautiful one; a dream that can

come no more, yet I am glad that I have had it.   I would that I had a flower her hand has touched—a glove or a ribbon she has worn !   Could I but know, that on my dead face such tears as hers might fall !' he added as he gave way to his dismal thoughts, and sooth to say his other circumstances were dreary enough.

The pouring rain had long since extinguished all the camp and bivouac fires, and was adding to the miseries of the wounded and the dying.   He had covered his horse with a blanket, and made a pillow of his holsters, and, with the flaps of his Servian forage cap tied over his ears, lay there sleepless and heedless of whether he was kicked, or trampled upon, by his charger's hoofs, or the hoofs of. others, while ever and anon the deep thunder grumbled over the spur of the Balkans, and the red lightning flashes lit up vividly, for a moment, the waters of the fast-flowing Morava, and a strange tower close by—a tower of human skulls, erected to commemorate a victory over the Servians by the Turks under Comourgi.

CHAPTER XIV.

A MYSTERY.

T was six in the morning of the following day. From the eastward came a blaze of glorious sunshine; the rain had ceased about midnight; the blue sky overhead was cloudless; shadows strange and darkly defined fell to the westward from rock and tree; the Morava was glowing in golden light; but by its margin lay the battle-field with all its horrors—a place that no sunshine could brighten.

Cecil was roused from sleep by Captain Mattei Guebhard, who announced that General Tchernaieff required his presence at head-quarters forthwith.

'For what purpose?' asked Cecil.

'How can I tell!' was the sulky rejoinder; 'you will learn when you get there.'

The truth is, that this Mattei Guebhard, who was—justly, as events proved—cold in the king's service, had been unhorsed in one of the charges on the previous day, and had come a little scurvily out of the action, having failed to rally or reform his troop; thus, though he dared not to sneer at Cecil, he was jealous of the honours he had won, but never could have conceived how little the ex-Cameronian valued them.

There is perhaps more hate at first sight in this world than there is love at first sight; and somehow Mattei Guebhard felt a curious hatred of Cecil, who was aware at the same time of having a most decided repugnance of him. Yet they exchanged cigars, and picked their way across the battle-field, where the dead were being buried in trenches; the peasantry were stealing arms and whatever they could lay hands on; where the scared vultures were hovering, angry and expectant, overhead; and where all the hedgerows, hollows, and ditches were, as usual in every battle-field, strewed with those mysterious scraps of papers, that are the sport of the passing breeze.

What they are, no one cares to inquire, not even plunderers and burial parties, who fling them contemptuously aside, after searching the pockets and other repositories of the slain. They may be only Orderly Room reports, and parade returns; but too frequently they are the last letters from mothers and sweethearts, or wives—letters full of love and prayerful tenderness, to those who can peruse them no more.

It was the first general action that Cecil had ever been in, and the field to him looked awful, in the sweet bright morning sunshine; and the idea occurred to him, that if it be true—and we cannot doubt it—that to the Creator the fall of a sparrow is not a matter of indifference, what must that of a human being be? Yet, there they lay in thousands, butchered, hacked, and in some instances torn out of the semblance of humanity, by cannon shot and shell.

'Here we are!' said Guebhard, gruffly, cutting short his reflections.

In a tent, round which a lancer guard was posted, dismounted, and leaning on their horses, with some staff-officers about him, Tchernaieff was seated at a table, and was in the act of sealing a long and official-looking blue envelope. Close by lay the body of a favourite staff-officer, for separate interment. A sheet covered it, and the dull outline of the profile, and the up-turned feet, showed plainly and ghastly to the eye. A veteran soldier, of great experience, and much stateliness of manner, he received Cecil politely and cordially, shook his hand, proffered his handsome silver case of cigarettes, and then said,

'To business.'

A portion of the letter was to the effect, that he had appointed Cecil to serve on his staff, as an extra aide-de-camp, *vice* Colonel MacIver, popularly known as 'Tchernaieff's Scotchman,' who had joined the Russian army at Kischineff; and his first duty in his new capacity was to be the bearer of despatches to Belgrade; and Cecil bowed, and muttered his thanks and gratitude.

'This packet contains my report of the battle,' said Tchernaieff, with military brevity, rising to end the interview ere it was well begun; 'the casualty lists, and, more than all, my *plan* for our further operations, if approved of, by his Majesty the King.'

Guebhard's face was a study for a painter as he heard all this, in the background, with hawk-like eyes, and ears that quivered, so intently did he listen.

'You will take the road by Resna and Paragatin,' said the General, speaking pointedly and emphatically; ' speak to none on the way ; save for what you want—food and fresh horses ; let no one join you on any pretence, or attempt to turn you from your path.   Here is the route chalked out for you, the seven towns through which you have to pass, ere you reach Belgrade.   Remember and be wary, as I have found you brave and trustful.'

'Take this ring,' said Count Palenka, coming forward, and drawing a valuable Russian diamond from his finger : ' I cannot give you gold medals or crosses like the King or his excellency the General ; but I may insist upon your wearing this, as a personal gift from myself—the gift of gratitude for a life gallantly saved at great peril.'

Flattered by the high trust so suddenly reposed in him by Tchernaieff, Cecil, for the first time since he had set foot on Servián soil, felt his heart fill with something of the fire of his wonted ambition ; but he knew not that he was selected, as a stranger, for this perilous and important duty ; and still less, perhaps, did he know that there was a rival and pretender to the throne of Servia, in the person of Prince Georgeovitch, who had scouts, adherents, and secret supporters everywhere.

He looked at the war-map, with which every staff-officer was furnished, and saw that the distance between Belgrade and the temporary head-quarters of Tchernaieff (who next day was to begin his march to Alexinatz) was, in all, about a hundred miles, as the crow flies, through a wild, disturbed, and rather lawless country, by steep, rough, and heavy roads; yet, if tolerably well mounted, he hoped to perform the duty, and overtake the army, in four days at the latest, and this he said laughingly to Pelham and Stanley as he bade them adieu, and, quitting the camp, disappeared on the road to Resna.

The army advanced ten miles to Alexinatz, where a daring *alerte*, culminating in a regular foray, was given to the Turks within their own lines; but several days passed on, and became weeks, without Cecil re-appearing at head-quarters. He left few behind him to surmise as to the cause of this—still fewer to regret him, though all believed that he must have been cut off on the way—but how?

'I shall be deuced sorry, if that poor fellow comes to grief,' said Pelham; 'he seemed a gallant soldier, and every inch a gentleman. Curiously reticent about his antecedents, though ; he laughed seldom, and when he smiled, did so as if smiles belonged to his past rather than his present life ; but that he was an army man was evident—he had all the cut of it.'

'Had—don't talk in the past tense yet,' replied Stanley ; 'he told us he had been under fire in India.'

'Has left the service under a cloud, perhaps — was the scapegrace of the family, probably. My family has one: I was that evil spirit in mine.'

'Any way, I do wish we had him back.'

The two Englishmen eventually offered a handsome reward in Austrian ducats for some intelligence regarding their missing comrade ; and it came, vaguely, to the effect that two wood-cutters, three weeks back, had seen a mounted officer, answering to the description of Cecil, attempting to ford the Morava near Palenka, about forty miles off, and struggling with its current just as the sun went down, an event in these lands followed by instant darkness.

'Near Palenka ?' said Captain Guebhard, with a frown, and then a cunning smile, as if questioning himself.

'Did he fairly cross ?' asked Pelham.

'Who can say ?' replied Guebhard; 'and if so, why has he not returned ?'

'Were the bodies of a man and horse found in the river ?'

'The wood-cutters said no; but I'll ride to Palenka and make inquiries, if Tchernaeiff accords me leave,' he replied, turning away.

'Why is *he* so solicitous in the matter ?' observed Pelham; 'his dislike of our absent friend has been pretty apparent to me.'

'The devil only knows his object; but I don't like his smile.'

'With his cunning black-beady eyes and bistre-hued visage, this Guebhard reminds me of a half-nigger fellow who was gazetted to the Dragoon Guards, when I was in them before joining the Coldstreams. We were anxious to get rid of him; but he was sly as old Nick, slippery as an eel, and cautious as a lawyer. At last one evening we all came to mess with our faces painted copper-colour or black, and with huge stick-up collars, to the astonishment of the waiters and of him too ; but he took the hint, and sent his papers in to the Horse Guards next day.'

So Cecil's fate remained as yet involved in mystery.

But that Guebhard did get leave ' to search' was evident, as the two Englishmen saw him quitting the camp soon after, attended by two or three mounted Montenegrins, melo-dramatic looking cut-throats, armed with rifles, pistols, and yataghans, clad in tattered garments with sandals of cow-hide, unkemped, unwashed, black-bearded, and ferocious in aspect.

' By George !' said Pelham, ' I should not like my *safety* to be looked after by such fellows as these !'

CHAPTER XV.

ON DUTY.

AFTER carefully loading his pistols, and scrutinising closely the trappings of his horse, a fine, fleet and active animal, Cecil bade adieu to the army of Tchernaeiff, and took his way westward on his lonely mission.

But for his forfeited position (forfeited, as he had always felt, by no fault of his own) and lost love—the lost life as it seemed—how exciting and joyous, to a young and ardent spirit, such a task as that he had in hand, with such adventures as it promised in wild Servia, would have been; for Servia, though nearly half the size of Scotland, is yet a kind of *terra in-cognita* to the world of Europe generally.

'What will be the end of it all for me?' he thought, as he looked around him on the strange land to which he had come to begin life anew—the world again.

Yet his spirit began to rise in spite of himself, as he proceeded at a hand gallop in the pure morning breeze, and he felt that life was not without some zest after all.

Here and there great forests bordered the way, with little valleys opening between, wherein, as being warm and sheltered, the tobacco-plant is cultivated. The country seemed lonely generally; more than once, however, groups of wild-looking and well-armed peasantry and workers from the salt and copper-mines, passed him; but during this part of his journey he met with nothing exciting, save at the little town of Tjuprga, for so it figured on his map, though he utterly failed to pronounce it, and into which he rode just as the sun, a great round globe of fire, was sinking behind the hills.

On repairing to the only *cafane* or hotel in the place, he found a Russian dragoon officer taking his departure therefrom, and prior to doing so, about to lash with his heavy whip a pretty little waitress, whom he accused of cheating him out of two copper piastres.

This was more than Cecil could endure; he drew a pistol from his holsters and called to the Russian to face him; but, muttering something about 'an island cur,' the gallant Ruski spat at his feet in token of detestation, and galloped away.

'And I am the comrade of wretches such as this!' thought Cecil, as he dismounted and found that he had accomplished thirty-five miles of his journey.

After a repast of hashed duck and caviare (having, as usual there, to use his own clasp-knife and pocket-fork), and after a bumper or two of strong red wine with the natural soda-water, which comes from many springs in Servia, Cecil lit a cigar, and, divested of his arms and tunic, gave himself up to reflection—and, sooth to say, he had as usual plenty to ponder over—while watching the sunlight fading out in the little street of one-storeyed houses, mere huts built of white-washed clay, and which he knew were too probably without beds, tables, or chairs, and furnished with little more than an iron pot, in which the inhabitants cooked, and out of which they ate everything.

Carefully securing his door against intrusion when night fell, he slept on a divan with his rug and cloak over him and his sword and pistols under his head for a pillow; and next morning, after settling his bill for a few copper piastres (one hundred and twenty-eight of which go to one British sovereign), he was again in the saddle and pursuing the road to Bratisna.

The next day saw him without any incident—somewhat to his disappointment, certainly to his surprise, at least. After passing through Kolar, and then Semendria, as his horse was breaking down, he was compelled to halt there for the night, within twenty-four miles of his destination. But the halt was not without interest, as there for the first time he saw that river so famed in history, the magnificent and dark-blue Danube, the waves of which 'have witnessed the march of Attila, of Charlemagne, of the Lion of the North, and the armies of imperial France; and whose shores have echoed to the blast of the Roman trumpet, the hymn of the pilgrims of the Cross, the wild halloo of the sons of Islam, and whose name is equally dear to history and to fable.'

Reining up his horse upon a slope, he watched the river for a time, flowing there between mountains clothed with forest trees, its blue waters in the vista washing in some places beaches of yellow sand, with pretty, toy-like hamlets sleeping in the sunshine, and then rode in to Semendria, which occupies a low peninsula in the river and is overlooked by a quaint old castle, in remote ages the abode of the kings of Servia, and which has since been taken and retaken, battered and bombarded by Turks and Hungarians in turn.

Next morning saw him approaching his destination, the stately city of Belgrade. Towering over its picturesque masses, over the spires and domes of more than a hundred Greek churches and Moslem mosques, steeped in the blaze of the morning sun on one side, and with deep shadows on the other, rose its citadel on the summit of a precipitous rock, surrounded by a lofty wall with flanking towers, a triple fosse, and a magnificent esplanade, four hundred yards in breadth.

On the summit waved the Servian tricolour, pale-blue and red together, with the white outside.

Around on every side spread lovely gardens. As he approached this famous frontier city, the scene of so many bloody sieges, Cecil could not but smile, in these our days of vast projectiles, at remembering how great a feat it was thought of the Scoto-Austrian Marshal Loudon, when in 1789 he opened his first parallel there, at one hundred yards from the glacis. That stately citadel was the scene of many

awful atrocities perpetrated upon Christians, and Cecil ere he left it was shown
the place where Rhigos the Greek was
sawn asunder limb by limb; and so lately
as 1815, thirty-six unhappy Servians,
among them the grandfather of Count
Palenka, were impaled alive, in violation
of a pledge given for their safety.

Anxious to return and to be rid of his
despatches, Cecil certainly did not loiter,
and in a few minutes he found himself
traversing the streets of timber-built
houses, and those lines of open wooden
stalls which compose the shops, the barber
and coffee vendor alone having glazed
fronts, and where the nationalities are so
distinctly marked in the motley population,
the laughing shopkeeper in his tiny
Servian bonnet, the suave insinuating
Greek banker or merchant in his red skull-
cap, and the haughty, sallow and bearded
armourer, blacksmith, or baker, always
Turks, as their white turbans show.

His national uniform, the time and the
cause—news of battle—a great victory

over the 'Turkish dogs' by the Morava,
spread like wildfire, and Cecil had no difficulty in finding his way to the palace of
the prince, or, as he was then universally
named, King Milano, which is simply a
handsome house with back and front
gardens, near the War Office, on the boule-
vard leading to the Semendria road, which
is bordered by double rows of trees.

As Cecil approached this edifice, important though his mission, some delay occurred in his presentation, as a Circassian
Prince with six hundred horsemen—all
wild-looking and picturesque Tcherkesses,
had just come in to join the standard of King
Milano. He was a very handsome young
fellow, wearing a busby of black Astracan
fur, with a coat of the same material (worn
over a shirt of the finest linked mail), with
a row of cartridge tubes across the breast
of it ; his sabre blazed with precious stones,
and he wore a pair of white kid gloves that
would have done credit to Regent Street.

Then came Cecil's turn, and by officers
of the staff, wearing blue coats and red

trousers, and French kepis with waving plumes, he was ushered into a stately apartment, and was graciously received by Milano, who gave him his hand to kiss, and read the despatches aloud to the group around him, with considerable emphasis and the most intense satisfaction.

Photographs have made all so familiar with pictures of the Servian King, that no description of him is necessary. Suffice it, that he was all the more warm in his reception of Cecil on discovering that he was a Briton, and learning the services he had performed in the recent battle. Milano was then in his twenty-second year, having been born at Jassy in 1854. He spoke French with fluency, having been educated at Paris, where his studies were interrupted by the assassination of Michail Obreno-vitch in 1868, after which he was pro-claimed Prince of Servia by the Council of Regency.

Replies to the despatches would be given Cecil forthwith, and meantime an aide-de-camp was desired to conduct him to the

Krone Hotel. There, weak and weary with his long and rapid journey, Cecil gladly flung himself upon a divan, and after a repast, made terrible by the inordinate seasoning of red pepper and red capsicums, or *paprikas*, with a bottle of Negotin claret, made from grapes that always grow on stony soil, he began to enjoy himself at an open window which faced the Gardens of Belgrade, which are certainly very beautiful.

Servian officers and Servian ladies were promenading there, or eating sweetmeats at marble tables, and reading the Servian *Istok*, while the band of the Royal Guard played in the gardens, and now and then the national air of 'La Belle Serbe' was called for and greeted with applause.

To Cecil, the people seemed pleasing in aspect; their eyes were blue or hazel, with chestnut hair and oval faces that were generally smiling. The men, tall, robust, and handsome; the women, slender, delicate, and all wearing graceful head-dresses.

Lovers were loitering there, and flirtations were in progress, as they are everywhere all over the world, and many were there who seemed happy as the yellow-throated bird that sung in a mulberry tree close by where Cecil lingered over a cup of coffee and a cigarette, and thought of the newness of his surroundings, and the strangeness of his fate, and his purpose in being there — if he had a purpose at all !

It was strange—passing strange ! In that field by the Morava he set no store upon his life—not even for Mary's sake, as she was lost to him as completely as if she were dead—yet how many who had circles of relations and friends to deplore them, and who doubtless set all necessary store upon their own lives, had perished there, falling ' as the leaves fall when forests are rended.'

Was he the same Cecil Falconer, who, but four months before, had been marching to the drums of the Cameronians ?

An end was put to his reverie by the appearance of the aide-de-camp, who brought him the king's despatches, and that evening he quitted Belgrade. As he gave a last glance at the wayfarers who loitered about the streets and at the doors of the cafés, cigarette in mouth, with their richly inlaid swords and long pistols stuck in their showy scarves, and with muskets slung behind them, looking very picturesque—he thought they would, at the same time, be unpleasant fellows to meet in some lonely place in a land where police are scarcely known.

He took a farewell glance of the Danube, studded with tiny villages, their churches and minarets, with Servians on one side fishing in curious little boats, Hungarians on the other tending their flocks, with vast mountains towering in the distance, and then rode quickly on what was now his homeward way.

Continuing his journey along the left bank of the Morava, the close of the second day found him, as he supposed, within thirty miles of Deligrad (from which

General Tchernaieff had moved to fight his victorious battle), when it became painfully certain to Cecil that he had too evidently taken a wrong path and lost his way, in a very lonely district, where few persons were to be seen, and where neither his German nor Italian availed in making inquiries.

Of the Roman road he had been pursuing—a road old as the days of Trajan—all traces had disappeared, and he found himself in a narrow forest path, overshadowed by huge pines, where he would be certain of *not* finding a guide, as such places are avoided at night, as being the haunt or abode of the *vilas*, evil spirits who can assume all shapes, but especially that of the cuckoo, according to Servian superstition.

Hence it was, perhaps, that two woodcutters whom he saw, fled at the approach of a mounted figure, looming tall in the forest—and these were the men who pocketed the Austrian ducats of Pelham and Stanley.

Fires glowed redly here and there upon the distant hills—doubtless from copper and iron mines ; but twice, isolated rockets described their fiery arcs athwart the darkening sky; what this might indicate, he knew not ; but urged his horse onward by the narrow path, which descended abruptly now.

He thought he could hear the murmur of a great current—the flow of a river ; but could discern nothing then, between the stems of the trees, or in the starless sky overhead—for in Servia the twilight —the gloaming, as the Scots call it—is very brief, and when the sun goes down, utter darkness, with amazing rapidity, envelops all the scenery.

Now an involuntary cry escaped him, as his horse, though at a walk, toppled heavily forward, and before he could respire a second time, he and it were both immersed in the current of a dark and rapid stream, too evidently the Morava.

The bank over which they had fallen was too steep to make the least attempt to return that way possible.　He took his feet from his stirrups, held up his horse's head, and guiding it gently with the stream. and towards the other side, uttered an exclamation of joy, as he felt its feet touching the ground.　But ere he left the stream, the trunk of a tree that came surging past, struck him from the saddle ; yet he clutched his reins, and stumbled ashore, bringing the horse with him.

He was safe, but, after a brave man's natural emotion of gratitude to God for that safety, a cry of dismay escaped him, on finding that his sword-arm hung powerless by his side.

It had been dislocated by the force with which the tree had struck him.　In a wild and unknown place, he was now helpless as a child, and something very much akin to consternation fell upon him.

CHAPTER XVI.

THE CASTLE OF PALENKA.

WHILE his heart sank within him, at the idea of being so suddenly rendered helpless and unfit for active exertion, in such a place and at such a time, his first thought was to ascertain that Milano's despatches were safe and dry. With difficulty he found that they were so, in his sabretache, and after putting fresh cartridges in his pistols, to be ready (though one handed now) for any emergency, he took his horse by the bridle, and somewhat disconsolately led it up a slope, towards where some lights were twinkling, high in the air above him, to all appearance, and about a mile distant.

Up, up the steep slope he struggled, by a path that led through an open gateway, and pursued a winding direction, till he reached a terrace or plateau, before a castellated edifice of striking outline and considerable dimensions, to all appearance the abode of some Servian magnate or landholder; but he was so faint with pain and exertion, that all he looked on seemed to be whirling around him.

An appeal to the knocker, a huge ring in the mouth of a grotesque face, brought a servant, a tall and robust fellow, in a species of livery, to the door, and by the lights in the vestibule that opened beyond, he stared with equal surprise and alarm upon the dripping visitor, who in a somewhat polyglot language, stated the predicament he was in. Another and another came, and ere long they made out that Cecil was an officer of the Servian cavalry—a messenger from the king, who had met with an accident; and as such he found himself rather abruptly ushered into an apartment of palatial aspect, where two ladies, an elder and a younger, were intent upon a game of chess, by the light of a large shaded lamp, the globe of which was supported on the shoulders of a silver statuette of Atlas; but both now arose with astonishment expressed in their faces.

Cecil at that time felt himself as if in a dream, or only half conscious of what was passing around him ; he remembered afterwards his words of explanation, the commiseration of their replies in the most softly modulated Servian (a soft language at all times) and he found himself committed to the care of ' Theodore,' the man whom he had first seen, and who proved to have been an old soldier, who had seen many broken bones in his time.

Cecil's sodden uniform was removed, and his hurt at once seen to, by the valet and an attendant of the lady of the house, who had been for a time one of the good sisters of the *Santas Kreuz Militar*, and knew precisely what to do, so fortunately for Cecil he was in good hands.

By them, gently, but firmly, the partial

dislocation of the arm at the shoulder—
fortunately it was only a partial one—was
speedily reduced, a process during which
Cecil nearly fainted.　Cloths dipped in
vinegar were then applied ; some wine was
given him, and soon after he was left to
repose ; but he, who had slept on the bare
ground for months past—though now in a
charming room and luxurious bed, with a
coverlet of rich silk lace, lined with pale
blue silk, surrounded by luxuries to him
unknown since he quitted Britain—felt
sleepless, and as the hours passed by they
were hours of pain and anxiety—pain to
endure, and anxiety to be gone on his
duty.

Great weariness weighed down his eye-
lids, and pain would be exchanged for what
he thought at times was a dream, or
sound sleep ; and as parts of the dream,
he saw the walls of a handsome room, a
little Greek oratory with a *prie dieu* before
it ; and therein the figure of some saint,
with a gilt halo of horseshoe-shape around
the head, and a tiny pink lamp burning

before it, and the girl, Ottilie, for such was her name, watching and flitting about it noiselessly.

She was more than pretty, with a violet-coloured velvet jacket, embroidered with gold, under which she wore a habit-shirt of the softest white cambric; and her dark sheeny hair was braided close round her small head, not under, but over a skull-cap of crimson cloth.

These, and other details, Cecil took note of next day, rather than on the night in question; and closing his eyes, he strove to collect his thoughts and think—think of what, or of whom, but Mary Montgomerie?

He was now to deem as past and gone for ever the love that made his veins to tingle and his heart to thrill in his bosom; yet he could not but remember with intense tenderness the last kiss she had given him, and the time—one of those, so some one says, that are given us by God to help us by the sweetness of their memory, in weary days to come.

She was so far away—so far away ! It seemed he could but think of her as the living do of the dead—perhaps as the dead may do of the living.

To him the slow hours were passed restlessly—almost without repose. 'There is,' says a writer, ' a strong contrast between a sleepless night and the first hours that follow it. Everything appears from so different a point of view ! The phantoms of night become again familiar objects, in the same way as in the region of ideas things gigantic reassume ordinary proportions. We fancy we are contending with the impossible, and find ourselves in presence of paltry difficulties. We believed that heroism was demanded of us, and find that it is simple duty we have to accomplish.'

So it was with 'Cecil when day dawned, and brought with it ideas that were practical.

Betimes came Theodore with hot coffee on a silver salver, which he proffered with a military salute, and the information that ' his excellency's ' horse had been attended to at the stables, and there was his uniform, dry and brushed to perfection, with his pistols and sword, burnished as only an old soldier could burnish them, for Theodore had served with the Austrian army in Bohemia, and been twice wounded at Sadowa, where his regiment was that remarkable one which perished nearly to a man under the new and terrible fire of the Prussian needle-gun; with all of which facts he informed Cecil, while re-dressing his hurt and assisting him to attire.

He also informed him of something else —that he was in the family residence of Michail, Count Palenka; and so, by midday, with his arm in a sling, Cecil expressed his anxiety to thank his hostess, the widowed mother of the count, for her kindness to him.

He announced himself as 'Sub-Lieutenant Cecil Falconer, of "Tchernaieff's Own," aide-de-camp on the staff,' and was ushered into the presence of the ladies whom he had seen on the preceding night.

'The preserver of my son's life in the battle by the Morava!' exclaimed the countess, coming forward and taking his left hand between both of hers, and gazing upon his face with humid yet beaming eyes.

'I only did my duty, madam, though the count was pleased to think I did more,' replied Cecil, 'and bestowed this ring upon me.'

'My birthday gift to my dear brother!' said the younger lady, laughingly.

'Your hand has worn it, then?' asked Cecil.

'Since I was a little girl in Vienna.'

'That enhances the value of it to me,' said Cecil gallantly, with a bow; 'but surely it must have been a world too wide for one of your fingers.'

'True; but I had it enlarged for Michail.'

Now, during the natural well-bred inquiries concerning his injury, and so forth, Cecil had opportunity for observing his hostess and her daughter Margarita.

The countess, though verging on fifty,

was still very handsome, for the Servian women, by their mode of life, can prolong their beauty beyond the average climacteric. She wore a long flowing dress of black cashmere, with a train behind, and confined at the waist by a silver girdle; a frill of softest muslin was round her throat, and a square of fine white lace arranged like a widow's cap was pinned over her head, with the ends falling on her shoulders. She had clearly cut features, soft dark hair lined with silver, fine eyes, and a shapely figure still.

Margarita was a womanly-looking girl of more than middle height, having a full and rounded figure of remarkable grace and elegance of bearing, set off by quantities of delicate lace and flowing drapery. Stately in walk and in every movement, she was a brilliant, flashing, and imperial-like beauty, with large and liquid eyes, a clear-cut aquiline profile, masses of rich, dark hair, and a small mobile mouth, with pouting, red and rather sensuous lips; and she was self-possessed, refined, and highly-bred.

Educated at Vienna—for Servia was long a province of Austria (after being shuffled backward and forward between the Emperor and the Porte)—she was highly accomplished, according to the European standard, and it was but too evident that she welcomed the advent of Cecil's visit—especially as a young Briton—for the women in Servia are reckoned as being quite inferior to the men, fit only to be the plaything of youth and the nurse of old age; a peculiarity of manners that has not arisen from four centuries of tyrant Turkish rule, but seems to be inherent in old Slavic custom, such as still appertains in Russia. But European ideas and fashions are now the rule at Belgrade, thus the country must change fast; and Margarita had been the reigning beauty when there as a maid of honour to the Princess Natalie, the wife of Milano, and daughter of a wealthy banker in Odessa.

The conversation soon drifted back to

the great Servian victory, and the narrow
escape of Count Palenka and the general.

'How courageous it was of you to risk
your life to save theirs; how self-devoted
to give Tchernaieff your horse!' said the
countess.

'It is not often a soldier has two such
strokes of good luck at once,' replied Cecil.

'Had you no fear for your own life—no
dread of dying?' asked the countess.

'No, madam.'

'Why?' asked Margarita, who had
scarcély spoken yet.

'Because it is as natural to die as to live
—to die as to be born; and life has now not
many charms for me,' he added, with involuntary sadness or bitterness.

'Now—had it more once?' asked Margarita.

'Yes—many—nearly all that I could
desire, contrasted with it now.'

'I grieve to hear you say so—you, with
life before you still,' said she, eyeing
him with growing interest, while slowly
fanning herself with a great round feather

fan, though the atmosphere was cool enough.

'You cannot leave this place for days yet,' said the countess, after a pause. 'Margarita shall write to the count and request him to tell General Tchernaieff of your accident. Meantime she and I will nurse you,' she added, with a kind motherly smile, 'and make you well and strong.'

Cecil sighed as he thanked her, and feared that his sword-arm would be useless for many a day; and indeed he was incapable of mounting a horse as yet.

CHAPTER XVII.

MARGARITA.

THOUGH named the castle of Palenka, the abode of the count of that name partook more of the character of a fortified house, as it had been built by his grandfather, an old heyduc, on the basement of a Roman or other ancient fortress, and had a legend connected with it, similar to that told of the castle of Skadra, that to propitiate the *vilas*, a beautiful young girl had been built up alive in the foundation of one of the towers; and Margarita, one day, showed Cecil the identical place in question.

All the rooms had parqueted floors,

polished like a coach - panel.   In the
dining-room, or hall, was a large round
table of massive form and baronial aspect,
and a lofty oak buffet, full of shining plate,
quaint crystal goblets, and quainter china.

The drawing-room was fitted up somewhat in the Turkish style or taste, for though
it had a grand piano and orthodox European
chairs, a low divan of yellow satin ran all
round it, and many of the most beautiful
objects of art that Vienna could produce
adorned it. Trophies of arms hung everywhere, many of them very old, many of
them collected perhaps by the veteran heyduc, who fought often in battle under Kara
George, and who was impaled at Belgrade ;
for here we may mention that these hey-
ducs were outlawed and deemed robbers by
the Turks, and like the Scottish caterans,
imagined that in setting law at defiance
they were only combating for a principle
of independence, and not acting dishonour-
ably ; and most of them, like old Michail,
the Heyduc of Palenka, made it their boast
that they robbed only the rich Moslem in-

vaders, but were generous to the Servian poor; and for military services to the House of Austria, his son was created a count by Francis I., the ally of Britain against Napoleon.

Cecil's mind was made comparatively easy by the fact that Margarita had written to her brother the count, detailing the mishap which detained him at Palenka; but the letter was never received, so he knew nothing of the mystery that enveloped his disappearance at head-quarters: and day followed day very quietly in that sequestered abode among the forests, and so far from any town.

The old countess, who had a truly Servian and holy horror of all strangers, thawed speedily to Cecil, and declared him one of the most delightful companions she had ever met, even in Vienna.

A thorough Servian of the old school, she was full alike of religion and supersti-tion, and observed most scrupulously the numerous fasts of the Greek Church—the four annual terms of abstinence, and every

Wednesday and Friday, and never uttered a holy name without crossing herself.

She was never tired of telling her beads, and if she awoke in the night when the wind was high, she trembled as she thought of the traditional vampire—a body which the Serbs supposed to be possessed by an evil spirit, which comes forth from the tomb of death to suck the blood of the living, till traced, taken, and burned to ashes. She believed in the existence of old Servian witches, who could steal away men's hearts, and close the wounds through which they had drawn them.

'I fear there are young witches in Servia who steal away men's hearts and leave the wound an open one,' said Cecil, who, but for the presence of Margarita, would soon have become intensely bored at Palenka, as the chief, if not only, visitor there was the pope or priest of the nearest village, a blue-eyed and long-bearded old man, who could only speak Serb, and whose demigod was the Archbishop of Belgrade.

Accustomed for months past to the

misery and wretchedness of the Servian camp, to Cecil, the dinner-table with shining white cloth, plate, crystal and ivory knives, under a flood of light from a rose-coloured chandelier, seemed the luxury of Sybaris; and for several days he had his food cut for him by old Theodore, or by the pretty hands of the girl Ottilie.

Both mother and daughter were intensely loyal in the cause of Milano and Servia, and hated the Turks as bitterly as ever the old heyduc himself could have done.

'It' was my brother Michail who recaptured the cross at Belina last year, as no doubt you know?' said Margarita.

'I was not in Servia then—what was the episode?' asked Cecil.

'It was in the famous battle of July. When the Turks ravaged Belina in Servia, they carried off a great cross from the altar of the church, and came on to the assault of our Servian troops, bearing it in front, and shouting, "You cannot fire on your God—you dare not fire upon your Prophet!"'

'And our poor Servians, rather than commit sacrilege, dared not fire, and stood perishing in their ranks!' said the countess.

'Till our Michail, at the head of a chosen band, burst, sword in hand, among the dense mass of red fezzes, recaptured the cross, and brought it into the lines of Milano, over heaps of dead and dying; and then—but not till then—did the Servians pour in a dreadful fire of shot, shell and rockets, beneath which the columns of the infidels melted away.'

When Margarita spoke, even with energy, as she often did, there was always something sweet and innocent about her, with a certain quiet dignity, and a touch of softness in her expression, which, when taken with the bright and lofty character of her beauty, rendered her wonderfully attractive.

She soon discovered that he was musical, and they sang frequently together, while she played the accompaniment; and when he gave forth the notes of the Master of Ravenswood's farewell to his lost love, and gave it with a power and pathos that, though she had heard many of the best tenors at Vienna sing the same air, yet none had seemed to do so with such tenderness and heart-broken despair—and when their eyes met, her heart began to thrill beneath the ardour of his gaze, for Cecil, when he sung thus, gave his whole soul to it, and thought of Mary—Mary Montgomerie only, or it might be the memory of the mother that taught him; but to the ear of Margarita every note seemed, as she once said, ' to be a lover's wail over a lost love.'

On one of these occasions, Cecil saw some pieces of dance music lying about, inscribed with the name of Captain Mattei Guebhard.

' The captain—he is a friend of yours ?' he remarked.

' He was here on a visit to Michail once —yes,' she replied, with a shrug of her shoulders, and dismissed the subject. ' I grew weary of him; he was jealous as Jelitza !'

But Cecil observed next day, that all

those particular pieces of music had disappeared.

Always fond of female society, Cecil found the daily association with this accomplished girl a source of the purest pleasure, and he strove, but in vain, to find traces and resemblances in her to Mary Montgomerie; for Margarita was larger, darker, more brilliant and colossal in her beauty, if we may use such a term.

She had quite a repertory of Servian legends, to which she recurred from time to time, and told with a piquancy which her foreign accent and foreign graces of manner enhanced; and one day she took him to a little lake—a dark and stagnant tarn, overshadowed by great trees, and near the Morava, which she affirmed to mark the grave of the jealous Jelitza, so famed in Servian song.

Remembering her reference to this personage when she spoke of Guebhard, he asked who she was.

'Oh, the very incarnation of jealousy!' said Margarita; 'she could not bear even

the brotherly tenderness of her husband
Paul for his young sister, and in order to
alienate him, slew his favourite courser,
and charged her with the act. But Paul
gave credit to his sister's denial. Then
she slew his falcon, and blamed his sister
therefor; but Paul would not believe her.
And at last she killed her little baby, and
left in its tender body a knife which Paul
had given his sister, whom he now slew in
the wildness of his fury, by having her
torn asunder by wild horses. But in the
end, the jealous Jelitza perished by the
same fate; and then we are told, "that
wheresoever a drop of blood fell from her,
there sprang up the rankest thorns and
nettles. Where her body fell, when dead,
the waters rushed and formed this lake so
still and stagnant. O'er the lake there
swam a small black courser; by his side a
golden cradle floated; on the cradle sat a
grey young falcon. In the cradle, slumber-
ing, lay an infant: on its throat the white
hand of its mother; and that hand a golden
knife was holding." All these apparitions

were visible here, once yearly, on this stagnant lake, till the days of my father, who had it blessed by the Archbishop of Belgrade, since when they have been seen no more.'

All the legends Margarita told him were wild and gloomy ; yet the Servians seemed to Cecil a lively people, and together they often watched the reapers singing merrily in the fields, and dancing, to the fiddle and native bagpipe, when work was over, the *kolo*, the national dance of the people.

Both were young and both were hand-some ; the acquaintance so suddenly begun ripened rapidly : but Cecil, unmoved by the brilliant attractions of Margarita, and by the perilous influences of propinquity, never for a moment felt. his heart waver in its loyalty to Mary, though he deemed her lost to him, and all other human love was dead in him now.

When the September evenings closed in, and the old lady, clad in costly velvet trimmed with beautiful fur from the Balkans, was reading her missal in a corner, Cecil and Margarita, if not at the piano, were generally seated close together—very close, an observer might have thought—at a tripod table of green marble, playing chess, he with his left hand, for the right was yet in a sling ; and watching, which he could not fail to do, her lovely little hand, so white and delicate, a very model for a sculptor, pushing the pawns and knights about, while all was still without, save the flow of the Morava on its way to join the Danube.

Between these two, when the countess was not present, we are compelled to admit that the conversation sometimes waxed perilous, notwithstanding Cecil's resolute platonism, when the large liquid eyes of Margarita, under their thick dark fringes, met his, and her scarlet lips, which we have said were rather sensuous, quivered and smiled, with an expression all their own ; and one of those perilous times was when, somehow, they fell on the subject of love—a natural one enough between a handsome young fellow and a beautiful woman.

'There are times,' said Cecil, after a pause, in reply to something Margarita had said, ' when men dare not love.'

'Dare not—when?' asked Margarita, as she made a false move, and had to play her king.

'I mean when to love is rashness, or would be presumption,' said he, thinking, as no doubt he was, of Mary and her vain old guardian.

'There may be rashness, but there is no presumption in any man offering his true and honest love to any woman—even a princess.'

'But would the princess accept it ?' said Cecil.

'Perhaps,' replied Margarita, looking at him with one of her smiles, and then drooping her lashes ; 'love is romance,' she added.

'Then I have lived the romance of my life,' said Cecil, a little bitterly, and perhaps unwisely, 'and have only its grim realities before me now.'

'Already—and you so young ?' she asked, with dilated eyes.

' Already !'

' I trust you mistake, and that romance may come again,' said she, softly.

' It is utterly past, so far as hope goes now.'

' Does the grass of the grave grow above it ?' she asked after a pause.

' In one sense — for my hope is buried.'

' I do not think any grave is so deep that we can bury in it all hope of another love and other happiness,' said Margarita, perhaps misunderstanding him, and making a rather leading remark, which Cecil—though not obtuse on such matters—failed, in his utter preoccupation, to perceive. Margarita bit her lip, and shoved her pawns about. She, accustomed to adulation and much admiration, was rather piqued by Cecil's coldness.

' All the world is alike to me now,' said he, rather absently ; but she gathered the conviction that he was neither married nor engaged.

' Are you so much of a misogynist that

37—2

you cannot even be the friend of a woman?'
she asked.

'I have not said so,' said he; 'nor am I
in any degree a misogynist,' he added, with
animation.

'Then you can conceive a friendship?'

'Yes, and a most tender one—and go
where I may,' he added, coming rather to
the point, as Margarita thought, 'I shall
never forget the friendship I have conceived
for you.'

'That emotion is not always a lasting
one.'

'Why—how?' he asked.

'Because it often ends where—love
begins,' she replied, with a laugh and a
downcast smile.

Cecil felt his heart beat quicker.

'Oh, by Jove!' thought he, 'this sort of
thing won't do—what must I say next?
This is making awful running, and I have
only been a fortnight here!'

But at that moment the countess, who
had dropped asleep over her missal, awoke,
and the conversation changed.

Truth to tell, Cecil was beginning to be somewhat scared, rather than flattered, by the brilliant *œillades* and rash speeches of Margarita. He did not quite understand the romantic impulses that came of her half-wild Servian blood, though partly tamed and tempered by a fashionable European education. She was totally unlike any other woman he had met before, and he could not determine to his own satisfaction whether she had conceived a secret fancy for him, or was only seeking to entangle him in a flirtation, for her own amusement, as she had perhaps entangled Mattei Guebhard and others before him.

CHAPTER XVIII.

CAPTAIN GUEBHARD.

WHEN Cecil thought of the despatches with which he had been entrusted by Royal hands, of the approved plans of the campaign which Tchernaieff anxiously and eagerly awaited; when he reflected, too, how he, a foreigner, a stranger, a humble and nameless volunteer, had been promoted, decorated, and honoured with high trust; and when he thought of the ready suspicion, jealousy, and mistrust of the Russians and half-oriental Servians of whom he was now the comrade, he groaned in agony of spirit over the helplessness which caused his detention at Palenka, and neither the society, the rare beauty, nor the blandishments, for it was fast amounting to blandishment—of the dazzling Margarita could console or wean him from the path of duty, or drown the sense of peril, perhaps, involved.

All the young men of Belgrade, and all the 'eligibles' of elsewhere, were with the army of Milano as officers or volunteers, all fighting the infidel Turks 'for freedom and Servia;' consequently, save the old pope, Palenka was without male visitors just now; and in the adjacent village, a place with a name not easily pronounced, it was 'noised abroad' that the strange officer who had so suddenly appeared at Palenka had succeeded in winning the heart of the beautiful Margarita, who had been hitherto deemed so unimpressionable by all, and it was thought not to redound much to the credit of the old countess, or to that of the youth of *La Belle Serbe*, that such a prize should be carried off without a struggle.

'The young Herr Lieutenant is playing

with fire here !' said the grey-moustached
Theodore to Ottilie, gloomily.

'How so ?' responded the girl, gaily ;
'is not youth the season for love ? and our
mistress is beautiful.'

'And manhood is the season for
marriage, girl ; but he dare not marry her,
and she dare not marry him,' he added
grimly, twitching his beard ; 'and I wish
him well away from Palenka !'

'Why ?'

'Because he is a fine fellow—every inch
a soldier—and I would not see evil come
to him.'

'Evil ?'

'I said evil, and I know—well, what I
know.'

The curiosity of Ottilie was piqued, but
Theodore was in no mood to gratify it.

To Margarita, Cecil was a species of interesting enigma. He had some sorrowful
past, which he carefully kept from her ;
she felt that instinctively, and she was
never weary of hearing him tell of the
places he had been in—India, Scotland,

England, and Italy—and smiled sweetly and softly at his descriptions of distant lands, that she had only heard of at school. She knew that he was accomplished, and the superior in education and ideas of any man she had yet met; thus, she admired and evidently liked him very much: but the villagers and the household were adopting conclusions too abruptly.

She had a perfect consciousness of her own beauty—a beauty of that remarkable type and quality which seems to belong to no country, so rare and striking was it—and, to enhance it, she had already decided that a few of her most becoming toilettes might be necessary for her purpose, which was no doubt to attract and dazzle, as she felt that his presence at Palcnka would greatly brighten the hours she deemed lost, by a temporary exile from Vienna, in consequence of her brother's presence with the army.

Preoccupied though he was by thoughts of another, and only anxious to take his departure, as he now hoped to do in a day or so, her coquetry became one day very apparent to Cecil, and it amused while it flattered him, as she invited his attendance on her at the piano.

On this day she had arrayed herself for conquest; and whether it was the well-assorted costume she wore and the subtle perfume of some fragrant flowers she held in a white and ungloved hand, or the soft light in her dark and liquid eyes, but Cecil thought certainly that he had never seen her look so piquante, brilliant, and lovely, with a loveliness picturesque and all her own.

She began to run her fingers over the keys, and then suddenly exclaimed, with a little laugh:

' Oh, this will never do !'

' What ?' asked Cecil, as he hung over her.

' I have been playing with one glove on —how absurd ! Please to help me off with it,' she added coquettishly, holding out her hand to him in a pretty, helpless way.

Such a tiny, lavender-tinted glove she

held forth to him to unbutton. Faultlessly it fitted the white dimpled hand, and reached far up the arm, with many little white buttons, the undoing of which was now the task assigned to him; and as he felt in his hand the firm, white, tapered arm, he saw a little mocking smile about her beautiful mouth; and, as their eyes met, something he read in hers made Cecil feel inexpressibly foolish. He must, he thought, say something tender—but why?

He was just undoing the last button, when Theodore came in with a card on a silver salver, announcing 'der Herr Capitän Guebhard;' and the figure of the latter was now seen looming darkly in the doorway, as he took in the whole situation and advanced slowly, with his spurs and sabre clanking.

'Playing with hearts, as usual,' said he, with a laugh that had no sound in it, as he took her hand and bowed curtly to Cecil.

'How dare you say so!' she replied, while a flush crossed her face, and an ex-

pression of irritation came into it for a
moment.

After a little pause, the visitor said,
after she requested him to be seated :

' I have just heard from old Theodore of
what had befallen the Herr Lieutenant. I
have also heard, but at head-quarters, that
he has important despatches from the King
to General Tchernaieff. There was a fear
that you had lost your way, or fallen into
the enemy's hands, and I volunteered to
come in search of you.'

' For that I thank you, Captain Guebhard ; and as for the despatches——'

' You will please to hand them over to
me.'

' Pardon me,' said Cecil, and paused,
while a dark gleam crossed the eyes of
Guebhard.

' How is your arm—well, I suppose ?'
he asked, with the slightest approach to a
sneer.

' If well, I should not be loitering at
Palenka.'

' You are nearly able to handle your

sword, I presume?' he continued, in a more marked tone, while playing alternately with the tassel of his sabre and his long black moustache.

'Very nearly, Captain Guebhard; but it is not the habit with British officers to bring their swords into a drawing-room among ladies.'

'Very likely; but I am a Servian officer, and I hope you consider yourself one now.'

There was something quietly offensive in the tone and bearing of Guebhard that irritated Cecil. The latter remembered the pieces of music inscribed with the monogram of the captain, and their disappearance too. He also remembered that Margarita had spoken of Guebhard's jealousy—that he was jealous as Jelitza, of the Servian legend and proverb; and Cecil thought there could be no jealousy without some love, or what passed as such.

What were, or had been, the relations between Margarita and Guebhard in past time—and how were they situated now ? That he came freely and installed himself as a privileged *ami de la maison* was evident, and as such he was warmly welcomed by the countess. But on what footing—·as a friend of the absent count, as the *fiancé* of Margarita, or as a relation of the family ?

So Cecil felt puzzled as well as irritated, and when again asked for his despatches, he plainly and firmly declined to give them up to Guebhard, though a superior officer.

'I fear I have interrupted your performance,' said the latter, abruptly changing the subject ; 'does the Herr Lieutenant sing ?' he asked of Margarita.

'Yes—with power and skill,' she replied promptly ; 'but when you entered I was just about to sing to him.'

'What ?'

'"The Wishes."'

Cecil urged her to begin, and placed the music before her, on which she sang both sweetly and effectively the little Servian song so-called, and of which the first verse runs thus, and is peculiar in its idea :

> ' " Oh that I were a little stream,
>   That I might flow—my love—to him !
>   How should I dance with joy when knowing
>   To whom my sparkling wave was flowing !
>   Beneath his window would I glide,
>   And linger there till morning-tide ;
>   When first he rouses him to dress,
>   In graceful garb, his manliness—
>   Then should he weak or thirsty be, '
>   Oh, might he stoop to drink of me !
>   Or baring then his bosom, lave
>   That bosom in my rippling wave !
>   Oh, what a bliss if I could bear
>   The cooling power of quiet there !" '

And as she sang, Guebhard, who doubted whether these six wishes referred to himself, listened and looked on with a visage, the lowering expression of which reminded Cecil of Hew Montgomerie under somewhat similar circumstances.

The captain of Servian Lancers had, as elsewhere stated, a silent manner and an unpleasant expression on his usually pale face, and analysis—not necessarily a very keen one—detected several defects in it. Among these, apart from his cunning black beady eyes, were thin cruel lips, and a general aspect of the face being perpetually a mask. He was not appearing quite to advantage just then, for if his manners were quiet, and generally polished, he had the stealthy gentleness and grace of a cat, and his bearing was suggestive of the adage that ' still waters run deep.'

He was a man of mixed race, and not a pleasant one to have, as Cecil felt him to be, a secret enemy; for he was half Italian and half Bulgarian, with a considerable dash of the Ruski. Cecil could little conceive how far his secret enmity was yet to carry him ; but he did not relish being reminded of his duty by Captain Guebhard, and still less to have hints given that he should soon leave Palenka behind him.

To allow the unexpected visitor to approach Margarita, and freely converse with her if he wished to do so, Cecil drew near to the countess and joined her in watching the reapers in a field, but he could not help overhearing, though said *sotto voce*, something that had reference to himself.

' Playing with hearts again, as I said before ?' whispered the captain.

'Don't be absurd!'

'I remember what mademoiselle was at Vienna.'

'Then your memory, like your sex, is—is——'

'What?' asked the captain, softly.

'Treacherous.'

'And so the Herr Lieutenant has been idling here,' said Guebhard, 'while we were enjoying ourselves by the Morava?'

'Enjoying yourselves?' asked Margarita.

'Yes — cutting up the Turkish dogs. Life is too short to let slip any opportunity nowadays.'

'Especially life in Servia—it is full of perils; and so you were solicitous for *his* safety? How kind!'

'I was solicitous to see you. I heard that he had been seen in the vicinity of Palenka.'

'By whom.'

'Some wood-cutters—so I made the excuse and came here.'

'Thus shunning your duties in the field?'

'Not more than he does.'

'With a disabled arm ?'

'For you to nurse,' replied Guebhard, with a smile on his lips and a glitter in his eye, that, had Cecil seen it, might have warned him of mischief to come ; and low though they spoke, he heard his despatches referred to more than once : thus he was scarcely surprised when he changed places with Guebhard and rejoined Margarita at the piano, that, under cover of a very brilliant sonata, she questioned him about them.

'Where are those despatches about which Mattei Guebhard seems so anxious ?' she asked.

'In my sabretache.'

'And it ?'

'Is in my apartment,' he replied, with surprise.

'As you cannot wear it constantly, take them therefrom,' she said, in an emphatic whisper.

'Why ?'

'They may be abstracted.'

' By whom ?'

'I do not—cannot say by whom,' she replied, with half-averted face.

' Do you suspect ?'

' Yes.'

And a crash on the instrument closed a conversation, on which Cecil resolved not to lose a moment in acting, and repairing to his own room, transferred the packet from the sabretache attached to his sword-belt to the breast-pocket of his uniform tunic.

He felt grateful to her for the interest Margarita had thus evinced in him, but he was sorely puzzled to know why Guebhard was so anxious to obtain the documents committed to his care; and he was soon convinced that her suggestion had not come too soon, when about two hours after he discovered the Servian captain in the act of quitting his—Cecil's—apartment.

'You here, Captain Guebhard ?' he exclaimed, with surprise and indignation in his tone, all the more so that he read a baffled and confused expression in the face of the other.

'Pardon me,' said he, bowing and passing on, 'but the dressing-bell has rung for dinner—I was in haste, and mistook your apartment for mine.'

It might be so; but Cecil thought it a curious circumstance that his belt and sabretache, which he had left hanging on the wall, were now lying on a sofa, and he smiled as he felt the packet safe in his breast, and resolved to secure his door for that night, the last he meant to spend in Palenka.

Cecil resolved to be in every way on his guard against this man Guebhard, and yet ere the night passed he was very nearly having a quarrel with him—a quarrel which, but for some forbearance on the part of the former, might have ended in a resort to pistols between them, after the ladies had retired and he and the captain were left to their cigars and wine; but the latter preferred raki, and under its influence he lost much of his subtle suavity

and oily politeness, and the real Bulgar in
his blood came out.

And, sooth to say, Cecil was not sorry
when the ladies did retire, for Margarita,
either to please and amuse herself, or to
tease and anger Guebhard, had addressed
the whole, or nearly the whole, of her
conversation to him, though it ran chiefly
on the progress of the war.

Lying or half-reclining on a divan, with
a rummer of raki and water at hand, a
cigar between his lips, and his cunning
almond-shaped eyes half-closed, though
they glittered brightly, Guebhard, after
some remarks about Margarita and her
singing, to all of which Cecil listened
silently, said :

'She is a dazzling girl—don't you think
so ?'

Cordially, Cecil admitted she was so.

'I wonder blood has not been shed
about her long ere this !' he exclaimed, in
a curiously suave yet vicious tone.

'Bah !' said Cecil, 'people don't fight
duels nowadays.'

'In your cold-blooded country, perhaps,' was the quietly scornful interruption.

'And we shall have daily blood enough spilt in other ways,' continued Cecil, without heeding him.

Guebhard drained his rummer, refilled it, and was not long in thinking of something else offensive to say, and gave each long, black, lanky moustache a vigorous twist, as if he gathered courage from the performance.

'You have not been idle while here, apparently, Herr Lieutenant,' said he, with one of his curious smiles, while carefully selecting a cigar from his case and proffering Cecil one.

'I do not understand you, Captain Guebhard,' replied the latter.

'You will understand this, that I heard your names — yours and Margarita's — bandied about in the common *cafane* of the next village.'

Cecil coloured with anger, but said quietly: 'We are not accountable for the gossip of the vulgar or the ignorant.'

'It is a pity, however, to compromise a young lady by your attentions, Herr Lieutenant.'

'Who *do* you mean?' asked Cecil, angrily.

'Who but Margarita Palenka?' replied Guebhard, suavely, but decidedly, emitting great circles of smoke from his lips.

'Compromise her?'

'I have said so, Herr.'

'With whom?' asked Cecil, endeavouring to suppress his annoyance; 'her mother or—you? I am here, like yourself, as a guest, and I do not recognise your right, Captain Guebhard, either to advise me, or suggest to me any line of conduct.'

'If I attempted to do so, it would be as your friend, and still more as the friend of Count Palenka's sister.'

Guebhard's voice was becoming thick under the influence of the fiery raki, and he sat for half-a-minute glaring at Cecil in a curious half-defiant and half-stolid manner, especially when the latter was not looking at him.

'At all events,' he said bluntly, 'General Tchernaieff expects you to report yourself in due course at Alexinatz.'

'Did he send you to me with this message?'

'No.'

'Then I require no advice from you, sir, as to any course I may choose to adopt.'

Guebhard's eyes glittered like those of a rattlesnake beneath their half-closed lids, and Cecil began to eye him back steadily and sternly.

'Captain Guebhard,' said he, 'to recur to the first matter in hand, the rumours at the *cafane*, what is your peculiar interest in the matter?'

'What matter?' stammered Guebhard.

'My intimacy—friendship—what you will, with the sister of Count Palenka?'

'Simply that I love her!' exclaimed Guebhard abruptly, with all the impulse of his really passionate nature; 'that I love her, and will brook no rival!'

'Then you need not fear me as one,'

said Cecil, laughing aloud; 'and if it will ease your mind, be assured that I had already arranged to leave this place to-morrow; my arm is so nearly well now, that I shall be able to reach my saddle with ease. And to end this rather absurd conversation,' he added, as he rose to retire for the night, 'be assured, I repeat, that on my honour you need fear no rival in me !'

'He lies, in his heart—the English dog !' thought Guebhard, as he silently gave Cecil his hand; 'and there are no lunatics like women, when an interesting foreigner comes their way. But I'll mar his wooing, between this and headquarters —by all the devils I will !'

'And you leave this to-morrow for the front ?' said he.

'To-morrow, by noon, at latest; and you, Herr Captain ?'

'I—I go on to Belgrade; but you ride by Resna ?'

'Yes.'

The captain, whose voice and steps were

alike unsteady, withdrew, and Cecil was not ill-pleased that they had parted without the quarrel which the other seemed anxious to provoke.

Next morning he found that the captain had quitted Palenka at an early hour, and soon after he was further to learn that Guebhard had *not* taken the road to Belgrade.

Ere noon next day, old Theodore was leading Cecil's horse, accoutred, to and fro before the door.

'We are so sorry that Palenka is about to lose you,' said Margarita, in her softest tone to Cecil, who had been saying some well-bred things, but in the genuine fulness of his heart, for the hospitality he had received.

'It is most kind of you to say so,' he replied, doubtful of how she might lead him on, for her eyes and manner were full of coquetry at the time.

'Don't you regret it?' she asked, with a would-be shy, upward glance.

'After all your kindness to me, a stranger, I should be most ungrateful not to do so!'

'But we may meet again,' said the countess, joining in the conversation.

'Perhaps,' said Cecil, with one of his sad smiles; 'but considering the chances of war, of life and events here, too probably never.'

Margarita stood by fanning herself, as she usually did. She knew that a fan suited well the style of her beauty, and she seldom neglected to display her skill in the use of one, and she had fans of all colours to suit her dresses.

So his sojourn at Palenka was ended now.

Intelligent and well read, Cecil was also master of that kind of small talk which marks a man of the world; and he had pleasantly wiled away many an hour with Margarita, the memory of which would haunt her in the time to come. It was a companionship, brief but pleasant, which she would be sure to miss, and to recall with genuine regret.

'She has been trying to lure me into a flirtation *pour passer le temps*,' thought Cecil, as he rode down the slope on the summit of which Palenka stood; 'and I am well rid—well clear of her alluring meshes.'

At a turn of the path he waved his cap in farewell, as he knew that her soft bright eyes were watching him from a window; but he knew not that from another point eyes were watching his departure in which a less pleasant expression might have been read.

CHAPTER XIX.

THE BLACK MOUNTAINEERS.

THE path by which he proceeded was narrow, rugged, often ascending rocky steeps and descending into rapid water-courses ; thus his progress was slow and devious. It was often bordered by forests of oak, ash and yew—the latter imparting a great gloom to the scenery ; it was overshadowed by hills, particularly those of Mount Mezlanie, with alpine peaks that were covered with thyme, rosemary, and other aromatic plants. Here and there he saw goats perched upon fragments of rock, their long beards waving in the wind ; and occasionally when the country became open, he passed bare fields whereon the oats and millet had been reaped.'

So he was once again in his saddle, with his sword by his side, his pistols in his holsters, and the world of wild life before him ! His pistols ? He thought it as well to look to them, and on doing so, found that the cartridges had been withdrawn from the chambers of both !

By whom had this been done, and why ? He could not suspect the old soldier Theodore ; but he did suspect Guebhard of tampering with some of the grooms. Forewarned thus, he at once proceeded to examine and reload them carefully.

As he rode on, he thought with more amazement than irritation of his conversation with the captain over-night, and of that personage's declaration of his regard for Margarita—his open jealousy, and threat of brooking no rivalry. Whether she had loved Guebhard in the past time, or whether she loved him still, was a matter of such little consequence to Cecil, that he scarcely thought about it at all.

'Could I,' he reflected—'could I but forget my own past, with its brightness and gloom—though the brightness was Mary, the gloom my mysterious disgrace—I might yet have some hope in the future here—even here ! My foot is already on the first step of the ladder, and military rank, perhaps glory itself, may yet be mine. I may yet gather one leaf of laurel, and who can say but that a corner in the Temple of Fame may await me too !'

He laughed at the thought. He was, in fact, too young to feel quite despairing yet. His spirit rose with the exhilaration induced by a rapid ride; and he at last began to think with ardour of the mess of the old corps, seeing his name in the public prints—the exultation and commendation of his pluck and bravery by Leslie Fother-inghame, Dick Freeport, and others—even his story going the round of the men's barrack; and more than all, of what would be the emotions of Mary Montgomerie !

Then, at the thought of her, be let his reins drop on the mane of his horse, and sinking into reverie—a reverie induced by the stillness around him—left the animal to proceed at its own pace, and even to pause, and crop the herbage by the wayside.

Never again, too probably, would the threads of their life cross, even for a moment, for Mary seemed as far removed from him now as heaven from earth. Then it would seem difficult to realise the idea that his life could pass on, unto the end, without Mary in it; and vaguely there would spring up in his heart the wild tumultuous hope that if he strove, even in this new and barbarous land, she might yet be his.

How often in the wretched Servian bivouac, through the long hours of weary night, had he lain under the stars communing in bitterness with his own soul, if we may say so; and out of the starlight Mary seemed to come to him vividly in fancy—Mary in her sweetness and loveliness, with all her gentle, soft, and winning little ways—her grace of movement, her tenderness of tone—the Mary that, too probably, he should never meet more.

Yet they had been so happy in their secret love of each other—the love that in its flush needs nothing more than to be mutual, 'though marriage seemed distant as death;' and as distant as that the former seemed now, though the risk of death was nearer than he thought.

Lost in reverie, he had proceeded thus a few miles, ere he became aware of the unpleasant fact that he had too probably lost his way, for the road-tracks diverged and crossed each other so frequently, and he met no one of whom he could make inquiries, till at a turn of the path he came suddenly upon two Montenegrins, who were on foot, under a tree, against which their muskets rested, and who were in the act of taking some food, each with the bridle of his horse over one arm.

Both were as repulsive-like men as one could meet, especially in a place so lonely, and the sudden appearance of Cecil seemed to afford them considerable interest. They were evidently two of the ' Black Mountaineers,' belonging to the body which served in the army of Servia, and they bore those arms which their race are never without, even in their most peaceful occupation : a musket, pistols, and yataghan— a short and sharply-curved flat sword, without a guard. They wore old and tattered garments of no particular colour, sandals of raw hide, were black-bearded, cunning, and forbidding in aspect—looking every inch like what the Montenegrins are in reality, savage barbarians, who in battle mutilate the fallen, and who never crave mercy, nor yield it, for when one is severely wounded, to save him from the enemy, his own comrades cut off his head.

As the language of these pleasant people is a dialect of the Servian, Cecil had not very much difficulty in making them comprehend the dilemma in which he found himself. They exchanged curious smiles, and then pointed out the way which led, they averred, to Resna.

Cecil gave them a few piastres; but, as he rode off, he saw them snatch up their muskets from the trunk of the tree, and in hot haste proceed to charge them, which they did somewhat slowly, as the weapons were old-fashioned muzzle-loaders. When again he looked back, both were taking deliberate aim at him over the saddles of their horses!

A double flash and double reports followed, and two bullets whistled past: one was flattened out against a rock, like a silver star; the other ripped some bark from a tree. And now, deeming discretion the better part of valour, while his heart swelled painfully with anger and indignation, he put spurs to his horse and drove it along at full speed.

Ere he could well reflect upon the course to pursue, two more muskets flashed out of the coppice ahead of him: 'ping! ping!' the bullets whistled past; they came from

rifled barrels, and he could see two more
mounted Montenegrins.

Cecil's heart began to beat wildly now;
he had no coward's fear of death, though
a great horror of being butchered thus,
helplessly and without defence. Yet he
was not without hope of escape; he remembered how many he had seen miss the
running deer at Wimbledon, and resolved
to trust to the heels of his horse : but soon
it cast a shoe, and the other began to
clatter, for evidently the nails had been
loosened !

The abstraction of the cartridges from
his holster-pistols, and this tampering with
his horse's shoes, he could account for now,
when remembering that the villain Guebhard had been in the stables betimes that
morning; and it was but too evident that
he had thus beset his returning path, and
these precautions showed that, notwithstanding the number of his followers, he
had a wholesome appreciation of Cecil's
pluck, skill and bravery.

Another shoe was shed; his horse began

to flounder now, and he heard the pursuing hoofs coming fast upon his rear. Cecil knew from experience the cruelty of which the Montenegrin nature is capable. He had heard, and seen, how Turkish wounded and prisoners had been shorn of their lips, noses, and ears, by the sharp yataghans of those so-called Christians, the Black Mountaineers, whose favourite household ornament is a Turkish head, dried in smoke; and who often bury their prisoners up to the breast and make targets of them at a hundred yards; and such a fate might now be his if he fell into their horrible hands; and he knew not how many were in pursuit of him.

It was not impossible that Mattei Guebhard had thus beset the road to cut him off, in a spirit of jealousy, rivalry, and revenge; but it seemed more probable that his present desperate and lawless proceedings had some mysterious reference to the interception of the despatches. This fact proved an alarming puzzle to Cecil, who longed, sternly, eagerly, breathlessly, to

have the captain alone with him, face to
face, and within range of his pistols.

In hopes to baffle pursuit, he had quitted
the direct road, or that which he supposed
to be such, and wheeled off by a path to
the left, but did so in vain, for they were
following him fast, and his horse, shoeless
now, failed to grip the loose soil of the way
with its hoofs alone.

Outriding the rest, two were now getting unpleasantly close to him, as the path,
a very narrow and winding one, began to as-
cend a steep spur of Mount Mezlanie.   He
rid himself of one of these by his pistol, but
as he wheeled round in his saddle to deliver
the Parthian shot by which he did so, he
felt in his right arm a maddening pang of
pain, and a cold perspiration burst over
him.

' God !' he exclaimed, ' if it is thus with
me now, how will it be if I come to use
my sword !'

The second Montenegrin, fast and far
outrode the rest, and without wasting time
in using rifle or pistol, he came thundering

full upou the rear of Cecil, whose horse, though fresh from the stable, after days of enforced idleness, and liable to resent the use of bit, curb and spur, was toiling up the steep and rugged path there was no quitting or avoiding. Cecil could see that it came close to the very verge of a precipice and then turned acutely to the left.

This he perceived just in time to save himself from a sudden and horrible catastrophe, by slackening speed, and guiding his horse, by bridle and knee, carefully round the perilous corner; while his pursuer, intent blindly on bloodshed and slaughter, came furiously up to the spot, and failing to turn the angle, being ignorant of it, or unable to check his speed, went over the precipice—headlong, horse and man—through the air, to find mutilation and death, where soon the vultures would be gathering, at its base, some hundred feet below.

His fate evidently made the rest more wary and caused some delay in the pursuit, which enabled Cecil to distance them considerably, as he pursued the pathway

through a solitary glen ; but he could see
that they were still keeping him in sight,
at a time when the afternoon was far advanced, and the darkness of a sudden
thunderstorm began to obscure both sky
and scenery.

CHAPTER XX.

AT this very time yesterday he had been hanging over Margarita at the piano, and busy with the numerous buttons of her long kid-gloves; and then listening to her coquettish song of 'The Wishes.'

Now what a change had come! He was a fugitive, pursued by men who were veritable human bloodhounds!

'No doubt about Guebhard now!' thought Cecil. 'Fool that I was not to quarrel with him at Palenka as he wished; and shoot him on the terrace, or anywhere else. But a time may come; nay, must come—if I escape—if I escape!'

And a time *did* come, when they were to meet face to face, though Cecil could little foresee, then, when and where it was to be.

It was plain enough that this subtle and ferocious fellow, half an Oriental, in the first moments of supposing himself supplanted by Cecil—already so successful in the field and camp—had resorted to the deep scheme of cutting him off and obtaining his despatches; spurred on by the intensity of the twin passions, love and hate—love for Margarita, and hate for a supposed rival, in more ways than one; and if successful, there was no knowing what foul stories he might circulate to blacken the honour of the dead, with Tchernaieff—stories that might ultimately find their way into every print in Britain!

To Cecil there was a bitterness worse than death in the thought of this; but he could little conceive that it was *not* for Tchernaieff, or any other officer in Servia, the fatal despatches and plan of the future campaign were wanted!

Cecil looked from an eminence; his pursuers were still in sight, but looking faint and distant, amid the gathering gloom.

' If it comes to the worst, I would rather be shot down than captured—could I be assured of being shot dead,' thought Cecil, as he rode steadily on, he knew not in what direction; he could make out that his pursuers were five in number, and one was evidently Guebhard. 'Had I a good Enfield rifle, I could pick every man of them off at leisure from this, and then there would be a few less Montenegrins to trouble the world.'

These fellows had belonged, of course, to that Montenegrin contingent, five hundred strong, which had come into the camp of General Tchernaieff; but he being an officer as humane as he was brave, had been compelled to expel the whole force for their barbarous mutilation of the Turkish wounded, and many of them were now prowling about as idle freebooters.

These Montenegrins—men of the race

which make such a stir in European politics at present—were literally savages of the *Zerna-gora*, as it is named, from the mountains clothed with darkest pine, which cover the greatest part of its surface—men inured to arms, hardship and cruelty from their boyhood—without religion or scruple, save in implicit obedience to their chiefs or leaders ; and in camp and out of it they committed many an awful outrage, the report of which never found its way into the columns of the *Glas Czernagora* or official journal of Montenegro.

Cecil knew that when leaving Palenka, he had, at the utmost, only some forty miles to travel, with a horse that was fresh and active ; but its shoes had been tampered with, he had been driven from his proper path, and the difficulties of that he traversed were now enhanced, as a storm came on.

Black and heavy clouds overhung the savage landscape—for savage it seemed, in its utter solitude. For the hour, the sky became preternaturally dark, and remained

so till night deepened ; and far in the hazy
distance the ghastly green forked lightning
flashed with weird splendour about the
peaks of Mount Mezlanie, and the thunder
boomed sullenly in the valleys below ; and
once or twice, when he obtained glimpses
of the winding Morava, its current seemed
increasing, as if in haste to leave the storm
behind it.

Then the heavy smoke-like rain came
down with a species of roar on the earth,
crashing through the foliage of the trees,
for hours after the time that should have
seen our wanderer safe within the outposts
of Tchernaieff ; but wild though the storm,
he welcomed it as a means of concealing
him from his pursuers, for he felt that if
overtaken, his arm was yet so feeble as to
make him rather helpless. He was compelled to ride slowly now, and with a firm
hand on a shortened rein.

The enormous pine trees towered sky-
ward like giants, and seemed to assume
something menacing in their aspect amid
the gloom. Knotted and gnarled stems

and roots also seemed to take the form of those grotesque monsters that figure in the forest through which Undine went; and in imagination perils mysterious and impalpable seemed to gather in the lonely path of Cecil, who was not without an active and fervid imagination.

At last he reached what appeared to be the border of the woodlands he had been traversing; the pathway grew broader; lights glittered out of the obscurity, and he could make out the form of a two-storied house, which he at once approached.

From the highway, as he supposed it to be, a modern gate gave access to a path through an orchard, as he eventually found, and in the centre thereof stood the house—the inmates of which, a Servian farmer and his family, received him with politeness rather than cordiality, and under the influence of the native distrust of all strangers, though he wore the brown Servian tunic of the patriotic army; but his pleasant and genial manner, and the fairness of his complexion won him favour, and while his horse was being stabled, he soon found himself installed before a wood fire, drying his sodden uniform, while the farmer's wife prepared some food, and her spouse endeavoured to describe the way he must pursue to reach the outposts of Tchernaieff, near Deligrad.

The house was a snug one. A tile-paved entrance-hall gave access to a room off it with four shuttered windows; it was floored with red tiles; an iron stove stood in a corner, and all round was a divan covered with rugs and cushions.

'Well,' thought Cecil, as some food was set before him, 'there are worse things in this world than taking pot-luck with a Servian farmer!'

Youth and hunger alone made him relish the plate of hot *paprakash*, or chicken soup with tomatoes dressed with hot pepper, bread, cheese, and black coffee *à la Turque*, served up in pottery, the form of which indicated a vast antiquity in its design—for the jars, vases, and plates, glazed white and green, were all Roman in style, and might have been used by the Emperor Trajan.

But little archæology was in Cecil's mind then; he was thankful to his hostess for the meal she gave him, and was intent on the host's description of the route he must pursue on the morrow, and was in the act of accepting from the hands of the former a tiny dish of the famous sweetmeat of Kirk-kelisie (near the Balkans), boiled grapes formed in a roll with walnut-kernels, when a strange sound like a distant 'whoop' caught his ear, together with the tramp of horses' hoofs. Then he felt his heart leap and his colour change, or fade.

'Horsemen are coming up the hollow way,' said a peasant, entering in haste.

'Horsemen!' exclaimed Cecil, starting up and looking at once to his pistols.

'Armed, too — Montenegrins — I saw them by a glimpse of the moon.'

'Guebhard and his gang—my pursuers. I am lost!' cried Cecil, leaping from the table and buckling on his sword, as he

looked hurriedly around him for concealment, defence, or escape.

His evident emotion and admission that
he had pursuers renewed at once the inborn
mistrust of the Servian household, who all
shrank from him. Despite his uniform and
the gold cross of Takovo, they imagined
he must be a culprit, and felt neither disposed to conceal nor defend him. Even the
gentle hostess eyed him now with horror,
mistrust and affright.

Cecil saw in a moment that he had
nothing to hope for from his host, or the
servants, among whom were four stalwart
Servians; and just as he heard the noise
of horsemen dismounting at the door, and
the unmistakable voice of Guebhard sum-
moning the house, he hurried away to the
upper story, and locking two doors behind
him, resolved with his sword and his pistols
to sell his life as dearly as possible.

By the noise and din below he became
aware that his pursuers had greatly increased in number, and now indeed a violent

death seemed close to him—terribly so, and his heart beat wildly.

'One can die but once,' thought he; 'and why should we shrink from what we cannot shun?' he added, involuntarily quoting Byron. If he perished in that obscure and secluded place, who would there be to regret him, save Mary? And then he thought of his comrades of the old Cameronians; but none would ever know his fate. There was something very bitter in *that* reflection, yet the memory of the regiment, and of his comrades, seemed to nerve him anew at this terrible crisis.

In the dark he sought about for furniture to barricade the room-door, if it was forced, and to form a baricade to fire over. A chest or two, a table and chairs, he piled against it, and then examined the window —it was small, narrow, far from the ground, apparently; but all was obscurity and darkness without, and unknown to him, there was immediately beneath it a deep hole, formed by the farmer when digging for copper ore. But now two minutes had barely elapsed, when shouts and execrations fell upon his ears, together with the din of blows upon the first door he had closed.

It was speedily beaten in, and then the door of the room was assailed. It seemed stronger, and for a time resisted the blows that were rained upon it.

'He wears a diamond ring, the gift of Palenka, which will prove a fortune to whoever gets it,' he heard Guebhard say in a loud voice; 'and he has a plan of the campaign, well worth a thousand ducats to me, and more to Kara Georgevitch !'

But his Montenegrins scarcely needed these incentives to outrage and bloodshed.

Through a hole in the door Cecil, for a moment, saw them crowding and jostling in the narrow passage, by the light of a torch held by one of their number. Ferocious-looking they were, yet men of magnificent physique, in long white camises, open in front, with gaudy waistcoats below; their sashes filled with knives, yataghans sharp as needles, and brass-butted pistols; their faces inflamed by raki, their dark eyes gleaming like those of devils; their white teeth glistening; their wide blue petticoat-trousers reaching to the knee, and their feet encased in thongs and sandals of hide.

A gleam of light flashed inward, as an axe clove a rent in the door, and thereat, for a moment, he saw the gleaming eyes and pallid face of Guebhard, and he fired full at it; but with what effect he never knew.

He fired again and again, at a venture, through the door, and so did his assailants; but their chance bullets went wide of the intended mark; while more than one shriek and hoarse malediction announced that his fire had told on the group wedged in the narrow space without; but now the door was yielding fast, and Cecil, aware that when once it was broken down he would inevitably perish by a death too probably of protracted mutilation and torture, threw open the window and resolved to drop therefrom.

Firing all the chambers of his revolver

at the door, through the splintered gaps in which a red light was streaming now, he lowered himself down, just as two of his assailants came rushing round a corner of the house, intending, no doubt, to cut off his retreat ; and quitting his hold on the window-sill, he fell down—down—he knew not whither ; but it was into the excavation already mentioned, and there he lay for some moments, stunned, confused, and well-nigh senseless, and incapable of further thought or action.

Round the hole, wherein he lay, his pursuers gathered.

'Here he lies !' exclaimed Guebhard, ' stunned or dead !'

' A single shot to make sure !' said one, cocking his long brass pistol.

' Not one !' cried Guebhard, imperatively ; ' I hear cavalry moving through the wood —perhaps those we might be sorry to meet. He lies still enough—some of our balls must have hit him—I saw blood in the room.'

That was the case certainly ; but it was

blood from the wounds of some of his own followers.

'Hark!' he added, as the sound of a cavalry trumpet was heard close by; 'here are shovels—cover him up—and when the horse are past, we can return and get what we want, at leisure.'

Cecil heard all this; he never stirred—scarcely breathed; and now he felt shovelful after shovelful of earth thrown upon him, cold, damp, and moist, as they proceeded, not to bury, but merely to cover him up, with the intention of concealing, as they thought, the dead body for a brief space.

No groan, no sigh, no sound, escaped him, while this horrible process went on; yet he felt a horror and dismay no language can depict, as he knew not how much soil they might heap upon him.

Unseen, or unnoticed by them, he eventually felt himself compelled to move his head, lest his face should be covered as completely as his body was; and then suffocation would ensue.

At last a great mass was shovelled in; his head was entirely concealed, and then Guebhard and his Montenegrins withdrew from the spot.

END OF VOL. II.

BILLING AND SONS, PRINTERS AND ELECTROTYPERS, GUILDFORD.

J. W. & Sons.